GW01006392

Henry's Upper Lough Erne in 1739

in a

LIMITED EDITION

of

660 copies

This is copy number

84

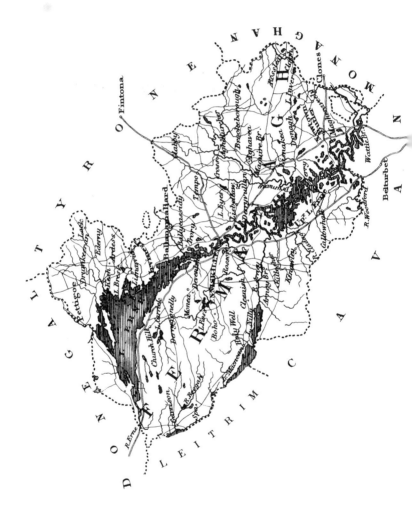

Henry's
UPPER LOUGH ERNE

IN 1739

Edited, with Notes and Appendices by
Sir Charles S. King, Bart.

With an Introduction by
Hugh Weir

BALLINAKELLA PRESS
Whitegate
Co Clare
Ireland

Additional material
©1987 Hugh Weir
Whitegate
Co. Clare
Ireland

ISBN 0 946538 10 7

The cover illustration is from
Ireland: its Scenery, Character, &c
Mr & Mrs S. C. Hall.
Vol III, facing p. 177

Reprinted
BOETHIUS PRESS
Kilkenny
Ireland

INTRODUCTION

This facsimile reprint of Sir Charles S. King's edition of the Reverend William Henry's fascinating description of Lough Erne comes about through my own family interest in the locality. Some time ago I acquired the late Earl of Belmore's copy which is still in excellent condition. Having succeeded in reprinting Lloyd's similar, but much less comprehensive, *Tour of Clare*, I felt that the demand for such works of historical, genealogical and topographical significance merited a reprint of *Upper Lough Erne*.

As in the case of numerous nineteenth century printed editions of earlier manuscripts, the copious notes and appendixes on the text by the editor are of equal significance, if not the major interest, for researchers and others. Sir Charles King did a wonderful job elaborating on so many of the families and places concerned. And there are large numbers of people throughout Ireland today who have at least some of their roots in Fermanagh, Cavan, and the other counties mentioned. Many of their family names are to be found in this book.

I thank Warren and Anne Loane of Enniskillen for their assistance. Our families are inextricably intertwined with those recorded herein. Indeed it is often said that 'everyone in Ireland seems to be related to each other'. This applies across the board irrespective of political, religious, or even cultural barriers. The staff of the Fermanagh County Library and Mr F. J. Nawn were also instrumental in locating the following information on Sir Charles King. I thank them also, and the Hewitt family of the Boethius Press, Kilkenny, for their excellent work of production.

Sir Charles Simeon King of Corrard, the third and last baronet, was born on the 8th December, 1840. His father, the Reverend Sir James Walter King, MA, and second baronet, was chaplain to the Marquess of Anglesey when the latter was Lord Lieutenant of Ireland. His mother, Anne Sophia King of Borris Castle, Co. Laois, was his father's cousin. Sir James died in 1874 and Anne Sophia in 1883. Of the six sons of the second baronet,

Sir Charles was the fifth. The eldest, James Walter who was born in February 1835, died in infancy. The second son, Lieutenant James Walter King, born the following year, was given his elder brother's names; he died unmarried at Calcutta in 1860, aged twenty-three. The Reverend Abraham Halton King died unmarried, aged twenty-four, in 1862. William Frederick King died in infancy in 1839, but as with the first and second born, his name was given to the youngest, and sixth, son, William Frederick King, ISO, FZS, Deputy Accountant General of the Navy, who was born in 1843. He died unmarried in 1909. There were two girls, Anna Sarah Sophia, who died in 1920, and Mary Matilda Elizabeth, who died in 1853. On 3rd June, 1891, Sir Charles married Sophia Louisa Davis, whose father was Lord of the Manor of Swerford and a Justice of the Peace.

As well as editing Henry's *Upper Lough Erne*, another of Sir Charles' works, published in 1906, was *A Great Archbishop of Dublin, William King, DD (1650-1729)*. This cleric, once imprisoned in Dublin Castle, was both kinsman to Sir Charles Simeon King, and to the present writer, whose forebear, Anne Weir of Hall Craig, Co, Fermanagh, married David King, Sheriff of Dublin (1716-17) in 1696. (A large quantity of the Public Records was secreted in David and Anne's house in Skinner's Row during the Revolution of the period.) Sir Charles Simeon King died on 3rd April 1921, and the baronetcy became extinct. It had been in existence just under a century, having been created for Sir Abraham Bradley King of Corrard, Co. Fermanagh, and Bloomsbury, Co. Dublin, on 6th April 1821.

I hope that many new readers will enjoy reading this valuable asset to the library of any Irish local historian, north or south. It is full of interesting pieces of information about people and places all over Ireland, and will no doubt contribute towards a greater understanding and awareness of a little more of our complex history.

H. W. L. Weir
Whitegate, Co. Clare
March 1987.

HENRY'S UPPER LOUGH ERNE.

HENRY'S

UPPER LOUGH ERNE

IN 1739.

EDITED,

With Notes and Appendices,

BY

SIR CHARLES S. KING, Bart.

DUBLIN:

WILLIAM McGEE, 18 NASSAU STREET.

———

1892.

[*All rights reserved.*]

PREFACE.

This " Description of Lough Erne," as the manuscript
is styled, is unfortunately imperfect, as the portion
describing the Lower Lake is missing, and a fragment
of the topography of the County Donegal, apparently
by the same author, has been inserted in its place.
The manuscript is now in the British Museum, cata-
logued " Add. MSS. 4,436," and is bound up with
other " Papers Relating to the Royal Society," originally
" E Bibliotheca Birchiana." Copied several years ago,
it has since circulated among friends, and is now printed
in the belief that it is of sufficient interest to appeal to
a wider circle of readers.

The author, the Reverend William Henry, a Fellow
of the Royal Society, was successively Rector of Killesher
and of Urney, and, in 1761, Dean of Killaloe; he was
M.A., 1748, B.D., and D.D., 1750, of Trinity College,
Dublin, and died 13th February, 1768; his remains
were interred at St. Ann's, Dublin, " 1768, February
14th. The Rev. Dr. Dean Henry, Chancel Vault "
(St. Ann's Register).

There being nothing interesting or archaic in the author's spelling and use of capital letters, these have not been retained.

Some appendices, and notes, genealogical and illustrative, have been added; they make no pretensions to contain full pedigrees of the families noticed, most of which may be found recorded in Sir Bernard Burke's " Peerage," &c., and " Landed Gentry," and some in Lord Belmore's " Parliamentary Memoirs of Fermanagh and Tyrone."

CORRARD, 1892.

ERRATA.

P. 35, note 4, line 1, insert before " Sheriff,"—*His grandfather, Col. Abraham Crichton, was*—

P. 59, note 1, line 23, delete " and," and insert *who*.

SUNSET ON LOUGH ERNE.

FAIR ERNE! It was an eve
Of glory and delight;
Of grandeur rarely seen,
Majestic as the night
Of Alpine skies, while linger yet the rays,
Which sunset's afterglow alone displays.

Brightly th' imperial Sun
Was beaming in the west;
Enrobing earth and sky
In glory ne'er exprest.
The smiling earth, admiring, blush'd with glad surprise,
And heaven adorn'd look'd down with wond'ring eyes.

The wid'ning lake did seem
A sea of liquid gold:
Enrich'd with glittering spoils
Of wealth and gems untold;
And every flow'ret on its banks that grew
Was changed and tinged with lustrous, golden hue.

The sky's deep azure-gold
Was toned with shades of night;
And pale and silver stars
Slept in the ambient light;
While radiant in the East, the moon arose,
To weave her spell of love at evening's close.

Then changed that gorgeous scene—
Softly the golden light
Faded to sapphire hue,
Save where, in radiance bright,
The moon the margin of the lake did tinge
And weave along the gold a silver fringe.

The stars in rapture woke,
To gaze upon the scene;
It seem'd too fair for earthly—
As Eden was, I ween.
It was a scene of loveliness more rare
In earth than heaven—'twas passing fair.

*　　*　　*　　*　　*

Slow fell the evening shades,
And all was hush'd to rest;
Save when some zephyr play'd
Upon sweet Lough Erne's breast.
Then tow'ring Cuilcagh* proudly threw his shade
O'er all Knockninny†, Lake, and glade.

J. W. KAYE.

DERRYBRUSK RECTORY.

* P. 42.　　† P. 46.

"All only for to publish plaine,

  "Tyme past, tyme present both;

"That tyme to come may well retaine,

  "Of each good tyme the troth."

THOMAS CHURCHYARD.

HENRY'S
UPPER LOUGH ERNE
IN 1739.

— ›♦‹ —

LOUGH ERNE.[1]

THE principal beauty of this county (Fermanagh) is Lough Erne.[2]

This lake—which is by far the longest in Ireland, and in several places spreads like a sea[3]—runs through the whole length of this county from the south-east point to the north-west, dividing it into almost two equal shares ; it neither takes its rise, nor terminates in this county, yet that there may be no interruption in the description, I shall here trace it from its sources to the ocean, and, as I go along, take in the principal rivers which flow into it, and the chief seats that adorn its shores.

[1] The Ordnance Survey Map of Upper Lough Erne will be found a useful companion to this work.

[2] Its ancient name is said to have been *Samhir* or *Samer*.

[3] It has a navigable course of fifty-two miles. The northern portion, or Lower Lake, extends from Enniskillen to Belleek, and is about seven miles in breadth across its broadest part—the author's MS. describing it appears to be lost—the southern, or Upper Lake, here described, stretching from Belturbet to Enniskillen, is about four miles across at its greatest breadth.

It rises from two heads:—

RIVER BALLYHAISE.

The more easterly is that which is commonly called the River of Ballyhaise, and by some Erne River; it rises in the south-east part of the Co. of Cavan from the large and beautiful Lough of Shariock; from thence it winds through the upper part of the Co. of Cavan, and passes a mile southward of Cootehill, whence circling through several pleasant valleys, it murmurs by Rathkenny, the seat of the Clements[1] family. Here the river is beautified by an elegant house, improvements and large plantations on the southern shore, and on its northern bank by extensive gardens and terraces.

---

[1] Its then representative, Theophilus Clements, Esq. (son of Robert Clements, Esq., M.P. for Newry, 1715, till his death in 1722, son of Robert Clements of Rathkenny, or Rakenny, who was attainted by King James's Irish Parliament, 1689), left issue a daughter and heiress, Anne, *m.* Rev. Edward Lucas, third son of Francis Lucas, Esq., of Castle Shane, Co. Monaghan, M.P., and had issue—Theophilus Edward, who assumed the surname and arms of Clements, and from whom descends the present Theophilus Henry Clements, Esq., D.L., of Rakenny.

The Right Hon. Nathaniel Clements (another son of Robert Clements, who was attainted 1689), M.P. for Duleek, 1727-1760, and for Cavan Borough, 1761, till his death, 1777; *m.* 1729, Hannah, eldest daughter of Wm. Gore, D.D., Dean of Down, and had issue two sons and four daughters—1. Robert, created, 1795, Earl of Leitrim; 2. Rt. Hon. Henry Theophilus, M.P., whose representative is Lieut.-Col. Henry T. Clements, D.L., of Ashfield, Co. Cavan; 1. Elizabeth, *m.*, 1750, Francis Burton, second Baron Conyngham, from whom the Marquises Conyngham; 2. Hannah, *m.*, 1752, Geo. Montgomery, Esq., of Ballyconnell, M.P. (p. 24); 3. Catherine, *m.* Gen. Eyre Massey, first Baron Clarina; 4. Alice, *m.* (his second wife), 1773, Gen. Sir Ralph Gore, sixth Baronet, created Earl of Ross.

Abraham Clements was a Crown tenant, in 1668, for 1,470 acres in Co. Cavan.

Hence continuing its course through the parish of Drung—a well inhabited country—it breaks in a cascade before the front of Ballyhaise,[1] the seat of Col. Brockhill Newburgh.[2]

This seat, for beauty and magnificence, may vie with any in Ireland. There is an ascent to it by several

[1] " Bally-Haize " in MS.

" It were also to be wished that even our gentlemen would in their country-seats imitate Colonel Newburgh, a great improver in the Co. of Cavan, who, as well as several others, does not only use stucco work, instead of wainscot, but has arched his fine dwelling-house, and all his large office-houses, story over story, and even all their roofs in the most beautiful manner without any timber."—*Reflections and Resolutions Proper for the Gentlemen of Ireland*, &c., by Sam. Madden, D.D., 1738.

[2] The patentee, in 1609, of Agheeteduffe, *alias* Ballyhaise, 1,500 acres arable, in Barony of Loughtee, was John Taylor of Cambridge, gent., who *m*. Anne ——, and was succeeded by Brockhill Taylor, Esq., M.P. for Cavan Borough, 1634, till his death, 1636, who left two daughters, co-heiresses—Eliza, born 1625, and Mary, born 1632, one of whom *m*. —— Newburgh, and brought Ballyhaise into that family. Thos. Newburgh, of Ballyhaise, Esq., was, with his two eldest sons, attainted 1689; he had, by his first wife, Mary ——. I. Thomas, *d. s. p.* (will dated 1696). II. Col. Brockhill Newburgh, M.P., Cavan Co., 1715-1727, *m*. Miss More of Salestown, Co. Kildare, and *d*. 1741, leaving issue four sons and two daughters—1. Thomas, of Ballyhaise, *m*., 1743, Charity Julia (*d*. 1745), daughter of Henry Blake of Lehinch, Co. Mayo, Esq., and *d*. 1776, *æt*. 83, leaving issue ; 2. Brockhill; 3. Wm.; 4. Arthur, *m*. Florence Cole, granddaughter of Sir Michael Cole, Knt.; 1. Maria, *m*. James Sanderson, Esq., of Clover Hill (p. 26); 2. Mary Anna. I. —— a daughter, *m*. Rev. Wm. Greene, of Dresternan (p. 14). Mr. Thos. Newburgh, senr., *m*., secondly, Letitia (*vivens* 1715, a relative of Dr. Edwd. Synge, Abp. of Tuam), and had by her a son Henry, *vivens* 1716.

Ballyhaise passed by purchase, early in the present century, to the Humphrys family. " Ballyhaise House, the seat of Wm. Humphrys, Esq., is a spacious mansion with an elevated front, curiously ornamented with arches."—Lewis's *Topog. Dict. of Ireland*, 1837. Wm. Humphrys, Esq., J.P., is the present proprietor.

terraces from the river, which are adorned with ponds, *jets d'eau*, fruit, and flowers.   The house is about 140 feet in front—it is made to last for ever—the roofs and all the apartments being vaulted, and curiously finished with stucco work ; and yet scarce any house in Ireland has so brisk and lively an aspect—the just mixture of the brick and hewn stone, and the proportion of the parts adding life to one another ; the large court and offices also behind it are all vaulted.   It is not easy to pass by this fine seat without delaying at it ; but to do justice to the house, its various apartments, gardens, vistas, avenues, circular walks, roads, and plantations rising to the tops of all the hills around, would require a description that would draw me too far from my present design.

The river forming a lovely meander around these improvements, in a silent, deep channel, continues its course for four miles through a valley diversified with small rising hills, meadows, and woods, to Butlersbridge, a little village on the great road, three miles north from Cavan.

Half a mile below that bridge, at the old church of Urney, it enters into an arm of Lough Oughter ; just as it enters this lake it receives a small canal which flows from a chain of several beautiful lakes in the form of oblong basins that are continued up to Farnham,[1]

---

[1] " One of the noblest ornaments of the county, for though the house does not possess much exterior magnificence, it is surrounded by a demesne of nearly 3,000 acres, comprising the richest pastures and the greatest variety of scenery adorned with wood and water, and everywhere improved by art.   Lough Oughter on one side of it spreads out from under the woods of Killy, and encircles many beautiful islands crowned with the finest timber."—Lewis's *Topog. Dict. of Ireland*, 1837.

the seat of John Maxwell,[1] Esq. The round hills that swell over these basins are for the most part clothed with woods or large plantations, divided by spacious vistas into a variety of pleasant ridings.

The course of this river, from its source to its entering Lough Oughter, is about twenty miles.

LOUGH GOWNAH.[2]

The western head of Lough Erne is Lough Gownah. It lies southward from the village of Scrawby (or

[1] M.P. for Cavan Co., 1727 till 1756, when he was raised to the Irish Peerage as Baron Farnham; and his second son (by his wife, Judith, daughter and heir of Jas. Barry, of Newtown Barry, Co. Wexford, Esq.), Barry Maxwell, was elected in his place; the latter succeeded to the Barony on the death of his brother, Robert, and was, like him, advanced to the higher dignities of Viscount, and Earl, of Farnham; he *m.*, first, 1757, Margaret (*d.* 1766), second daughter and co-heiress of Robert King, of Drewstown, Co. Meath, Esq., and had issue—1. John James, second Earl, born 1760, *d. s. p.* 1823 (when the Barony reverted to the issue of the Hon. and Rt. Rev. Henry Maxwell, D.D., Bishop of Meath, third son of the first Baron); 1. Lady Anne, *m.* 1787, Col. Richard Fox, of Fox Hall, Co. Longford (*d.* 1833), and *d.* 1801, leaving issue. 2. Lady Judith, *d. unm.*, 1818. Earl Barry, *m.*, secondly, 1771, Grace, daughter of Arthur Burdett, Esq., of Ballymaney, and *d.* 1800, leaving by her two daughters—Lady Grace, *m.* Sir Ralph St. George Gore, Bart., and Lady Elizabeth, *d. unm.*, 1782.

Henry, seventh Baron Farnham, who, with his wife, perished in the fearful accident on the North-Western Railway, near Abergele, 20 August, 1868, compiled and published his *Royal Descents, from Henry III., Edward I., &c., and from Robert Bruce,* 1850; his brother, Lieut.-Col. Hon. James Pierce Maxwell, M.P. for his Co., 1843-65, the present, and 9th, Baron Farnham, has also succeeded to the Nova Scotia Baronetcy of Calderwood, Co. Lanark, created 1627, on the death of his kinsman, the tenth Baronet.

[2] "Gawney" in MS., *i.e.*, "the Lake of the Calf."

It is about 214 feet above the level of the sea, and nearly thirteen miles south-west of Cavan. "The meaning of the name is explained by a legend which describes the origin of

Scrabby), and washes the south-west part of the Co. of
Cavan, and part of the Co. of Longford; it stretches
between them for about three miles in length, and one
in breadth. Though the country around is not improved, the lake is naturally very beautiful, having
several pleasant islands, a gravelly shore, the land rising
easily around, and the skirts in several places shaded
with woods.

On the north shore of this lake stands Cloon—a small
hunting lodge belonging to Arthur Cecil Hamilton, Esq.,
in a little peninsula almost in the form of a star, having
several woody points shooting out into the lake. It is
not safe to be particular in the several agreeable prospects which this well-chosen lodge affords, lest a just
description should carry too much the air of a romance.

From the eastern end of the lake, at the village and
old castle of Scrawby (or Scrabby), flows a small river
which runs on the south-east side of Bruce Hill, through
a coarse country for eight miles, to the back of Lismore
Castle—an handsome, new-built seat of Thomas Nesbitt,[1] Esq.—pleasantly situated and adorned with extensive plantations. Half a mile lower at the bridge of
Ballyhillan it enters

Lough Erne. There is a well in the townland of Rathbrackan,
one mile from Granard, in the Co. Longford. In this well
once lived a magical calf, which was kept enclosed in it by
means of a door, which all persons using the well were strictly
enjoined to close after them; but one day a woman going to
draw water forgot to shut the door, and the wonderful calf
jumped out, the water following him, expanding its course as
it went, so that neither calf nor water stopped their race till
both leaped into the sea at Ballyshannon!"—*Ballyshannon*, by
Hugh Allingham, 1879, p. 10.

[1] M.P. for Cavan borough, 1715, till his decease, *circa* 1750.
He acquired his Cavan estate by his marriage, 1713, with Jane,
daughter and heir of Arnold Cosby, Esq., of Lismore Castle

Lough Oughter.

Lough Oughter[1] signifies " The Upper Lake," and is so called to distinguish it from the other part of Lough Erne, which spreads below Belturbet ; it consists of a great number of branches, or rather a collection of lakes, which divide the country that lies between Cavan, Kilmore, Killeshandra, and Belturbet. The interspersion of this lake—the rich verdure of the soil—and the many little hills rising in the forms of hogs' backs, many of them skirted with wood—render this by far the best and most beautiful part of the county of Cavan.

At the distance of a small mile from the upper end of this Lough, on the very ridge of one of these small hills, stands exalted the episcopal seat of Kilmore.[2] Though it be a single seat, without any town or village adjoining, it makes a specious appearance. The house

(Capt. of a troop of Iniskilling horse, 1689), and had issue, with three daughters (of whom Jane, *m.* Thos. Burrowes, Esq., of Stradone House, Co. Cavan, and had issue ; and Elinor, *m.* Rev. Wetenhall Sneyd, of Cavan, and she *d.* 1754), six sons, of whom Cosby Nesbitt, born 1718, succeeded both to the family estates and to the representation of the borough ; he *m.* Anne, daughter of John Enery, Esq., of Bawnboy, and left issue. His descendant, the late Alex. Nesbitt, of Lismore, and of Oldlands, Co. Sussex, D.L., *d.* 1886, leaving a widow, Cecilia, daughter of Capt. Frederick Marks, R.N.

The immediate ancestor of the family, Alexander Nesbitt, of the House of Dirleton, Haddingtonshire (derived from Nisbet, or Nesbitt, of that ilk), settled in the Co. Donegal, and *m.* Alice, daughter of Alex. Conyngham, of Mt. Charles in that Co., Dean of Raphoe (*d.* 1660), ancestor of the Marquises Conyngham.

[1] " Owter " in MS., " 160 feet above sea level."—*Ballyshannon,* p. 10.

[2] " The Episcopal Palace, an elegant mansion in the Grecian style, has been recently rebuilt on a more eligible site near the former structure, which is about to be taken down."—*Lewis's Topog. Dict., Ireland,* 1837.

is long, lofty, and capacious, about an hundred feet in
length, and forty in width; it has two fronts: the
entrance is by the east side. The front is a large square
court, the south side of which is formed by the church,
the west by the house, the north by a wall'd enclosure,
through which passes the avenue planted on each side ;
from the east side, which seems open, there is a descent
by several steps into a spacious gravelled terrace covered
with spreading fig-trees, pears of the choicest kind, and
stone fruit, the other side adorned with pyramids of box,
yew, and holly: from this terrace descend steeply the
gardens replenished with various kinds of trees, roots,
and pulse ; they are divided into several quarters, and
the whole enclosed by an high stone wall. Below the
gardens lay, as an eye-sore, an irregular bog full of pits.
The late Bishop, Dr. Goodwin,[1] began in this a canal to
answer the hall-door; the present Bishop[2] has levelled
the whole bog, and, by grass seed, reformed it into a
beautiful meadow—for verdure and agreeableness not
inferior to a parterre ; the canal is completed, being
about 500 yards in length, and in the middle is widened
into a basin 100 yards over ; from the canal a plantation
of trees is carried on as an avenue to the tops of the
little hills beyond it, by which improvements that which
was naturally a nuisance is reformed so as to become
the principal beauty and ornament of this front.   The
western front opens into a gravelled terrace of about an

[1] Timothy Godwin, D.D., a native of Norwich, Bishop of
Kilmore and Ardagh, in 1714 ; translated to Cashel, 1727 ; died,
1729.

[2] Josiah Hort, a native of Gloucestershire, Bishop of Ferns,
&c., in 1722; translated to Kilmore, &c., 1727 ; and to Tuam,
1742 ; died, 1752 ; ancestor of the Baronets of Castle Strange,
Middlesex.

hundred paces long. From the terrace descends, in an
easy hanging level, a parterre agreeably diversified with
verdant sod, gravel walks, small fruit trees, elms, and
arcades of beech and hornbeam ; the sides are enclosed
with high brick walls covered with choice fruit trees ;
this parterre terminates in a deep ha-ha ; looking into
the centre of the parterre is a large shell seat adorned
with stucco. From the parterre is continued through a
beautiful meadow a spacious avenue of a triple row of
elms on each side, which, at the high road, terminates
in another ha-ha with piers : this beautiful field is at
some distance from the avenue on each side planted
thick with young trees. The whole—the verdure of the
meadow and parterre, the avenue, the walks, the terraces,
the house which is stuccoed—have an effect equally
grand and beautiful from the road. On the southern
side of the parterre lies another garden planted with
good fruit trees, and agreeably divided by tall hedges of
hornbeam and holly ; in one of these enclosures is a
physic garden ; the whole is enclosed with a high wall.
Within this enclosure stands the largest and most
perfect old Danish fortification in the kingdom ; it consists of two high mounds, each having a large platform
at the top ; they have in the middle a short passage to
one another ; the whole is encompassed with a high
dike and deep fosse, in which is a spring well ; this
fortification is agreeably transformed into a pleasing
retirement—the top of the dike being smoothed into a
circular terrace, the fosse planted with limes, easy spiral
ascents being made to the tops of the mounds, the platform of one planted with firs, the other with elms, and
having yews planted in the forms of easy chairs to read
on. Between this garden and the south-west angle of

the house stands a venerable old grove of sycamores—
planted an hundred years ago by Bishop Bedell—the
largest of them stands in the middle of the terrace and,
from thence, spreading its boughs into the churchyard,
shades its planter's tomb! The front of the house lay
formerly naked and neglected; but the present Bishop,
observing it most capable of ornament, has caused by
these several improvements its beauty to be displayed.
The south end of the house looks into the churchyard,
and from it the church goes off in right angles, being
contiguous, and having a communication with the house.
That door[1] (way) of the church which looks into the
churchyard has been a beautiful piece of ancient carving;
the stones are now so worn with time that many of the
figures are defaced. The church has been much adorned
by the present Bishop, who has sashed it, flagged it,
pewed, and painted it. At the south angle of the
churchyard, within a small wall'd enclosure, are de-
posited in a vault the remains of the good and great
Bishop Bedell,[2] over which is raised a tombstone with

[1] This richly sculptured Norman doorway was taken, it is
believed, from the Abbey of Trinity Island, in Lough Oughter.

[2] A native of Black Notley, in Essex ; Fell. Emmanuel Coll.,
Cambridge, 1593 ; B.D., 1599 ; Provost, Trin. Coll., Dub., 1627 ;
Bishop of Kilmore and Ardagh, 1629 ; resigned Ardagh, 1633.
This zealous divine regarded himself as not merely the pastor
of the British colonists in his diocese, but also of the sadly
neglected native Irish. "How is it?" asked the eloquent
Puritan, Dr. Owen, of the assembled Commonwealth Parliament, on the Day of Humiliation, 28 Feb., 1650—"How is it
that Jesus Christ is in Ireland only as a Lion staining all His
garments with the blood of His enemies, and none to hold Him
up as a Lamb, sprinkled with His own blood, to His friends?
Is it the sovereignty and interest of England that is alone to be
there transacted? For my part I see no further into the
mystery of these things, but that I could heartily rejoice that,
innocent blood being expiated, the Irish might enjoy Ireland

his arms, and this modest inscription,—

> " Gulielmi Bedell Quondam Episcopi
> Kilmorensis Depositum." [1]

The present Bishop is now repairing the injuries which this venerable tomb has suffered by time. The north avenue, which leads up from the road to the seat, is, by the present Bishop, carried on beyond the road along the ridge of a hill, to the farthest point, from which there is an extensive prospect variegated with no less than nine large pieces of water. Though this seat fails in that regularity which shines in modern pieces of architecture—which are begun and executed by one plan—by reason of its being begun by Bishop Whetnell,[2]

so long as the moon endureth, so that Jesus Christ might possess the Irish."

Bedell laboured earnestly for the benefit of the natives by circulating the New Testament in the Irish language, and also holding church services in the same tongue. " The Irish did him unusual honours at his burial," Feb. 9, 1641-42, " for the chief of the rebels gathered their forces together, and, with them, accompanied his body from Mr. Shereden's house, to the churchyard of Kilmore, in great solemnity, ... and discharged a volley of shot, and cryed out in Latin, *Requiescat in pace ultimus Anglorum*, for they had often said that as they esteemed him the best of the English Bishops, so he should be the last that should be left among them;" one of their priests also exclaiming, *Sit anima mea cum Bedello.—Life of Wm. Bedell, Bishop of Kilmore*, by Dr. Gilbert Burnet, 1685.

[1] In Mant's *Hist. Ch. of Ireland*, i. 569, appears an engraving of this tombstone, from a sketch made in 1820. An esquire's helmet surmounts the shield with the family arms, and above it is a mitre !

[2] Edward Wetenhall, D.D., a native of Lichfield, of an ancient Staffordshire family ; Bishop of Cork, 1679 ; translated to Kilmore, 1699 ; *died*, 1713, and buried in Westminster Abbey. He was one of the four Bishops summoned to attend King James's Parliament, 1689. Dr. King, Archbishop of Dublin, in a letter to Dr. Charlett, Master of University College, Oxford, dated 17 June, 1721, complains " as to those clergymen who are sent us from England, I believe it will not be pleaded that

on some ruins wherein Bishop Bedell lived, built up by
Bishop Godwyn, and beautified by this present Bishop,
yet, upon the whole, for convenience and agreeableness
of situation, it scarce falls short of any episcopal seat in
the kingdom.

On the east side of another pleasant hill, half a mile
northward from the Bishop's, stands the Deanery House
from which the hill descends in an easy hanging level;
it is behind well covered with large trees. A few paces
above it is a strong fort, which, being on the top of the
hill, commands a prospect of a great part of Lough
Oughter. In the late wars the Deanery House stood in
this fort, and was defended against King James's army,
under Galmoy, by Dean Dixie's[1] son and Lieut. Carleton,
who, being obliged to abandon it, and flee to Lough
Oughter, were taken; they were dressed up in beggars'
rags, and in this manner led, with their faces to the
horses' tails, to Belturbet, where, after being exposed to
the scoffs of the rabble, they were next day hanged on
the sign-post by the general's door, and their heads cut
off and given to the soldiers to kick about the streets as

they are the brightest, generally speaking, though I confess to my
observation they seem notably dexterous and industrious to
make money for their wives and children. Thus the See of
Derry was served by Dr. Hickman, my successor, who entirely
rooted up and destroyed a large flourishing wood, which I, with
care and cost, had planted whilst at Londonderry. Thus the
See of Kilmore was served by Dr. Whitnall, who sold a wood
belonging to his See, which, if standing now, would, as I am
informed, sell for £20,000. But instances of such sort are too
many to be mentioned."

[1] Edward Dixie, M.A., Dean of Kilmore, 1664, attainted, 1689,
and *died, circa* 1691.   His eldest son, Wolstan Dixie, Captain
of a troop of Inniskilling horse, was the victim of Galmoy's
treachery on this occasion, and his Lieutenant was Edward
Carleton, who shared his fate, March, 1688-9.   For the account
of Lord Galmoy's breach of faith, see Archbishop King's *State
of the Protestants of Ireland*, 1692, p. 177.

footballs; but the Inniskilleners, within a few days after, took a just and bloody revenge of these murderers.

In one of the most southerly bays of Lough Oughter, within a mile of Kilmore, stands Trinity Island,[1] so called from the ruins of an old church on the southern shore which is dedicated to the Trinity: it is a rich soil, and mostly covered with wood, which, as the ground of the island rises, appears to advantage. This island formerly belonged to the See of Kilmore, as appears by an inquest held in the reign of King James I., specifying all the lands and advowsons of that diocese. The record of this inquest is preserved in the Rolls Office; it has been since clipt off from the See.

About a league northwards from Trinity Island stands the strong old castle, Cloghoughter[2] — so called from a rock in this lake on which it is built. It stands about a quarter of a mile from the shore, and, as there is no ground now left but the site, the waves on all sides wash its walls. Within these dismal walls, and in a more

[1] In 1634 " Luke Dillon, Esq., of Trinity Island," was M.P. for Cavan Co.

[2] " Clogh Owter " in MS. Anciently the stronghold of the O'Reillys. " The only place," writes Dr. Burnet, " of strength in the whole county. It was a little tower in the midst of a lake (Killekeen), about a musquet shot from any shoar. . . . . The castle had been in the hands of one Mr. Cullum, who, as he had the keeping of the Fort trusted to him, so he had a good allowance for a magazine to be laid up in it for the defence of the country; but he had not a pound of powder, nor one fixt musquet in it, and he fell under the just punishment of the neglect of his trust, for he was taken the first day of the rebellion (Oct. 23, 1641), and was made a prisoner here."

Sir Hugh Cullum, or Culme (originally of Derbyshire), of Cloughoughter, Co. Cavan, Knight, M.P. for Cavan borough in 1613, m. ——, daughter of —— Emerson, of Derbyshire, and d. 1630, leaving issue four sons and three daughters—1. Arthur; 2. Hugh; 3. Philip; 4. Amadous; 1. Jane, m. Henry James, Dean of Kilmore; 2. Elizabeth, m. George Bradshaw, Gentle-

than ordinary severe winter, was the truly apostolical
Bishop Bedell detained prisoner by the popish rebels,
from the 18th of December, in 1641, till the 7th of
January (following). By the hard usage in this cold
place, but much more oppressed with grief for the
dreadful havoc daily made of his flock by the murdering
popish wolves, his strength was so impaired that he
died on the 7th of February at Drumcorr, a little farm-
house on this lake, belonging to one of his clergy, the
Rev. Dennis Sheridan.[1] This was a " meer Irishman,"
whom the good Bishop, in his zeal to promote the con-
version of the native Irish, had promoted to the parish
of Killasher[2]—at the present the benefice of the author.
He adhered firmly to his patron and benefactor in his per-

man, of Bradshaw, Derbyshire ; 3. Anne, m. John Edgeworth,
of Cranallagh, Co. Longford (Funeral Certificate in U. O.).

In this castle Lord Montgomery was confined by the rebels,
after the defeat by them of Monroe and the Scots' army, 15
June (1646 ?). Here died, by poison, as is supposed, 6 Nov.
1649, Owen O'Neil, a near relative of Sir Phelim O'Neil, and,
like him, a leader of the Irish, but, unlike him, a brave and
honourable soldier, who, from the time of his arrival with re-
inforcements from Spain, 1642, acted in accordance with the
rules of civilized warfare, and disavowed the atrocities committed by other leaders.—*Life and Times of John Leslie, D.D.,
Bishop of Clogher, &c.*, by Rev. R. J. Leslie. 1885.

[1] Dr. Burnet describes him as "an Irish minister, Denis
O'Shereden," who "had forsaken their religion, and had
married an English woman."

[2] In this parish is situated "Florence Court, the beautiful
mansion of the Earl of Enniskillen, which stands in a large
and finely planted demesne."—Lewis's *Topog. Dict., Ireland*,
1837.

The author's predecessor in this benefice, in 1719, was the
Rev. William Greene, of Dresternan, Co. Fermanagh, who was
attainted by King James's Parliament of 1689 ; Dr. Samuel
Madden's *MS. Hist. of Fermanagh*, 1718-1719, gives particulars
relating to him. He "purchased an estate in the said parish
(Killesher) from Sir James Caldwell, and built a handsome
house and chapel of ease as a burying-place for himself and

secutions, and ministered to him till his death. It must give pleasure to know the extraordinary reward which his pious gratitude and duty received from the Divine Providence. He lived Incumbent of this parish to a great yet vigorous old age, and saw two of his sons Generals in the Imperial Service; a third, Secretary of State, and Commissioner of the Revenue; a fourth, Patrick[1] Sheridan, Bishop of Cloyne; and the youngest, William,[2] Bishop of Kilmore and Ardagh.

family. His father (Marmaduke Greene, of Drumnisklin, in same County, who died 24 June, 1681), a gentleman of credit, married in ye worthy family of Creichton (Jane), who was sister to Coll. Abraham Creichton, of Crom, and mother to ye said Mr. William Greene, and to his brother, Capt. Abraham Greene (of Ballymacreese, Co. Limerick, *m.*, 1694, Annabella, daughter of Capt. Arthur Blennerhassett, and *d. s. p.*, 1724), who was a famous forward officer in ye late warrs. Mr. Wm. Greene's deceased wife was sister of Coll. Brock Newborough, of Co. Cavan (p. 3), and he has two sons and two daughters—1. Mr. Henry Greene (of Dresternan and Ballymacreese, High Sheriff, Co. Fermanagh, 1721), *m.* (1714) daughter of Capt. Richard Poirets (and *d. circa* 1745, leaving issue); 2. Mr. Brockhill Greene," *m.* Sarah, daughter of Hugh Montgomery, Esq., of Derrygonnelly, Co. Fermanagh, and *d. circa* 1736, leaving issue. The two daughters of Rev. William Greene were—1. Mary Greene (born 1685, *died* 8 Feb., 1762), *m.* Rev. James Cottingham, M.A.; and their eldest daughter, Elizabeth, *m.*, 1731, Charles King, of Corrard, Fermanagh, Esq.; 2. Jane Greene, *m.* Major Christopher Irvine, of Cooles, Fermanagh, ancestor of the present Col. John Gerard Irvine, of Killadeas, D.L., Fermanagh. "Mr. William Greene's grandfather was Mr. William Greene, who came (over) along with his relation, Sqre. Burley, and purchased a handsome estate in ye North, and married ye ancient family of Spenser, and of great relations. The coate of armes, three running stags in a gren field."

[1] A native of Cavan; Dean of Connor; Bishop of Cloyne, 1679-1682.

[2] A native of Cavan; Dean of Down; Bishop of Kilmore and Ardagh, 1681; though attainted by the Jacobite Parliament, in 1689, he remained faithful to the fallen dynasty, and was deprived, as a non-juror, of his bishopric in 1691. Archbishop King describes him, in 1704, as " exceeding poor and crazy;" he *died circa* 1717.

RIVER CROGHAN.

Westward from Cloghoughter there shoots out a spacious arm of the lough ; into this runs a small river, which takes its rise out of a large and beautiful lake lying between Killeshandra and Carrigallen, on the borders of the counties of Cavan and Leitrim ; thence taking a circuit, it flows by the castle of Croghan into a spacious lake eight miles in a circuit, resembling a bason, and filling up the whole space between Croghan and Killeshandra ; hence it steals out into another lake of the like form and dimensions, and thence into Lough Oughter.

LOUGH OUGHTER.

In a large peninsula—formed by this chain of lakes to the north and west, and by the arms of Lough Oughter to the east and south—stands on an eminence, to which there is on every side an ascent, Castle Hamilton,[1] the seat of Arthur Cecil Hamilton,[2] Esq. The imagination

[1] " Adjoining the town (Killeshandra) is Castle Hamilton, the seat of R. H. Southwell, Esq., a spacious mansion surrounded by an extensive and highly embellished demesne." —Lewis's *Topog. Dict., Ireland*, 1837.

[2] Sir Francis Hamilton, Knt., created Baronet (1628), of Kealagh, undertaker for 3,000 acres in Barony of Tulleknock, Co. Cavan, took an active part against the rebels in 1641, and was M.P. for Cavan Co. in 1661, and was then " of Castle Hamilton." His wife, Dame Elizabeth Hamilton's (*alias* Willoughby) will was proved 1664. His son, Sir Charles Hamilton, 2nd Baronet, *m.*, 1673, Catherine, daughter of Sir Wm. St. Paul (*alias* Semple), of Letterkenny, Knt., and died in 1689, leaving issue one son and two daughters.—1. Sir Francis, third Baronet, attainted, 1689 ; M.P. for his county, 1692, until his death. " The Hon[ble.] Sir Francis Hammilton, Barronett, was interred at Killyshandra, in the County of Cavan, February the 9th, 1713" (Funeral certificate, U.O.) ; he had *m.*, first,

cannot easily conceive the various agreeable prospects
of wood, water, hills, lawns, and plantations which on
every side encompass this seat. It has two fronts : the
western, which is the principal front, is extended about
200 feet ; before it is a spacious palisado'd ring, from
which an avenue, the whole breadth of the front, is
carried on through pleasant meadows, having a beautiful
lake on its south side, to the market-town of Killeshandra. The approach to this seat from the town is
by another large, winding avenue, shaded with huge
trees of an hundred years old, which is carried along
the rising ridge of the hill which descends from the
avenue, on the north side to the large bason before

Catherine, daughter of Hugh Montgomery, 1st Earl of Mt.
Alexander, by whom he had a daughter, who died young ;
secondly, Anne, daughter and co-heiress to Claud Hamilton,
Esq., but *d. s. p.*, when his two sisters became his co-heirs,
viz.—1. Nichola Hamilton, *m.*, first, Philip Cecil (*d.* 1684), of
Drumurry, Co. Cavan, Esq. (descended from Wm., Lord Burleigh,
Queen Elizabeth's Prime Minister, whose grandson, William,
second Earl of Salisbury, was father of Charles, Viscount Cran-
borne, who *d. v. p.*, leaving James, who succeeded his grand-
father and the aforenamed Philip), and had by him Arthur Cecil
Hamilton, heir to his maternal uncle Sir Francis Hamilton,
m., 1720, Anne, daughter and heiress to Thomas Connor, of
Dublin, and had two daughters—1. Margaret Cecil Hamilton,
m., 1741, Sir Thomas George Southwell, Bart., first Viscount
Southwell, and their second son, Robert Henry, Lieut.-Colonel,
8th Dragoons, purchased his maternal grandfather's estate of
Killeshandra, or Castle Hamilton, and *m.*, 1786, a daughter of
Dr. Moore, of Dublin, and had issue Robert Henry Southwell,
of Castle Hamilton, who *d. s. p.* ; 2. Nichola Cecil Hamilton,
m., 1750, Richard Jackson, of Fork Hill, Co. Armagh, and *d.s.p.*
Mrs. Cecil *m.*, secondly, Arthur Culme, of Lisnamain, Co.
Cavan, Esq. (attainted, 1689), and had issue by him Hugh
Culme, *d. unm.* II. Dorothy Hamilton, the second sister and
co-heiress to Sir Francis, *m.* Francis, son of Sir John Edgeworth,
Knt., and had issue John, *died unm.*, and Francelina.

The Castle Hamilton estate was sold, in 1844, by Robert
Henry Southwell, Esq., and its present proprietor is William
Joseph Hamilton, Esq., J.P.

mentioned, and on the south to another beautiful lake, which stretches near a mile in length from the site of the town. The entrance into this front is by a spacious stucco'd hall, properly adorned with Cornish pilasters and niches; this is reputed the largest hall in the kingdom, being forty-four feet in length, and in breadth thirty-four; the height is equal to the breadth; from this hall several doors open into the apartments. These lie chiefly on the south front, from which the gardens descend into a succession of long and spacious terraces to a large lake, on a small island in which, near the lowest terrace, stands a banqueting-house; these terraces are planted with choice wall fruit, and afford an extensive prospect of the town, country, and deerpark, which is beautified with several small pieces of wood and plantations; there are in it, hanging over the lake, some large fir near an hundred years old. From the house, the peninsula is continued beyond the deerpark, eastward, for a mile and a-half; in all this way are several spacious, open fields, descending to different arms of Lough Oughter, some on the north, others on the south side. On a verdant, rising hill at the eastern extremity of this peninsula is erected an octangular banqueting room, twenty-nine feet diameter, on each side a large window; in a line with each window a vista is cut through the wood that surrounds the bottom of the hill, which carries the eye to so many different branches of the lough. One of these vistas takes in Cloghoughter Castle.

From this place Lough Oughter is diversified into a great number of agreeable forms by a variety of islands, peninsulas, creeks, basons, and canals for five miles till it is again collected into a beautiful river a little above Belturbet.

The Erne.

This is a pleasant borough, charmingly situated on
the south side of the river, from which it ascends to the
top of the hill, in one straight and broad street ; from
the height another, forming with this a right-angle,
descends to the bridge ; at the angle formed by the two
streets stands a pretty market-house, which commands
a fine prospect of the whole town and river. A little
more southerly stands a large church, which is generally
crowded, all the inhabitants within the corporation
being Protestants ; and opposite to this, on another hill
over the east end of the town, stands a parsonage house.
In the late wars Colonel Wolseley,[1] while the Inniskilleners lay encamped here, fortified the churchyard and
parsonage house by a strong dike and fosse, and the
whole town by a line drawn between them. A little
below the parsonage-house, by the water-side, stands a
large barrack for two troops of dragoons.

On the top of the hill opposite the market-house,
stands the castle, the seat of Lord Viscount Lanes-

---

[1] William Wolseley, Colonel of Horse, appointed in July,
1689, Commander-in-Chief of the Inniskilleners, rose to the
rank of Brigadier, and became Master of Ordnance ; M.P. for
Longford borough, 1692, till his death, *circa* 1699 ; a Privy
Councillor and sometime a Lord Justice of Ireland. He was
youngest son of Robert Wolseley, Esq., of the ancient family of
Wolseley, of Wolseley, Co. Stafford, Clerk of the King's Letters
Patent, created a Baronet in 1628, and his wife Mary, second
daughter of Sir George Wroughton, Knt., of Wilcot, Wilts.

From the Staffordshire Baronets descend the Baronets of Mt.
Wolseley, Co. Carlow, from whom springs the distinguished
General, Sir Garnet Wolseley, K.P., created, 1882, Baron, and,
1885, Viscount Wolseley.

borough.[1] This is a lofty, square house, divided into several large rooms and apartments ; but its principal beauty and grandeur is from its bold and pleasant situation, and its hanging gardens, which descend in a variety of plats and terraces to the river, which, at the lowest terrace, is in the form of a broad and long canal, where generally some small pleasuring yachts and other boats ride at anchor. About twenty years ago this castle was struck in an extraordinary manner with lightning, the traces of which are preserved to this day, and seem to confirm that philosophical opinion, that, what the vulgar call the *thunder-bolt*, is only the focus of that stream of liquid fire which is then discharged. This thunder struck the top of the castle, close by the stack of chimnies, from which it shot down perpendicular to the bottom. The hole it made in the garret ceiling, through which it darted, is scarce three inches diameter. This seems to be the very focus ; from thence

[1] The Rt. Hon. Humphrey Butler, third Baron Newtown-Butler, second Viscount, and created, 1756, Earl of Lanesborough, in the peerage of Ireland, Sheriff, Co. Cavan, 1727, Cap. Battle Axe Guards, Governor, Co. Cavan, 1756 ; M.P., Co. Cavan, 1703-1713, Belturbet, 1723, till he succeeded to his father's peerages in 1735. He *m*., 1726, Mary (*d*. 1761), daughter of Wm. Berry, Esq., of Wardenstown, Co. Westmeath, and *d*. 1768, leaving an only son, Brinsley, second Earl, born 1728, from whom descends John Vansittart Butler-Danvers, sixth and present Earl of Lanesborough, Lieut., Co. Cavan.

Sir Stephen Butler, Knt., of Belturbet, the immediate ancestor of this family, was an undertaker, *temp.* James I., in Fermanagh, for 4,000 acres in half-barony of Coole, and 1,000 acres in half-barony of Knockninny (Geo. Alleyne's *Muster Roll of the Co. Farmanagh*, 1618), and in Co. Cavan for 2,000 acres, in Barony of Loughtee, M.P., Co. Cavan, 1634. He *m*. Mary, youngest daughter and co-heiress of Gervase Brinsley, of Brinsley, Notts. (she re-married Edward Philpot, Esq.), and *d*. 1639, leaving issue three sons and four daughters, and was buried in the chancel of Belturbet Church.

diffusing, it knocked to pieces the stone of the hearth, and cut to itself a circular passage about three feet diameter; descending to the next floor, and growing more diffused, it cut through the hearth and floor a passage of about eight feet diameter, from thence descending into the hall and spreading wide, it—by the violent concussion of the air—dashed down two stands of arms hung round the hall, and broke out of the door, tearing down one side of it; two women were in the hall—the one who stood on the further side, near the arms, was struck down astonished, but not hurt; the other, who was that instant shutting the door, was struck half-dead; that side of her next the lightning was left all black, the other not in the least discoloured; she, in a few days, recovered, and attended me at the time I observed this progress of the thunder.

This town lies very conveniently to trade, having the advantage of the carriage through the whole length of Lough Erne; it has considerable fairs for cattle, and is the principal mart for the linen manufacture of the counties Fermanagh and Cavan.

LOUGH ERNE.

From this town downwards the lake goes by the name of Lough Erne. Having passed the town, it changes its course northwards, and forms from the east end of the town an exceeding beautiful canal of a mile in length. It observes the like form of a large canal, with here and there a little winding, for six miles to the castle of Crum.

RIVER OF AUGHALANE, OR WOODFORD RIVER.

About three miles below Belturbet, on the west side,
it receives the River of Aughalane.   This river rises in
the southern part of the County of Leitrim, in the
parish of Cloon.   Thence it runs to Ballinamore, where
it turns great iron works; a little further it passes
through several large lakes, adorned with verdant hills
and great woods.   In a small peninsula that shoots out
from the most beautiful of all these basins, stands on a
little eminence the neat parish church of Drumreily.   It
lay in ruins for some ages, but is restored by the present
Bishop of Kilmore.   Hence, in a little more than a
mile, the river flows in a semi-circular form about
Woodford,[1] the seat of William Gore, Esq.[2]   This fine
seat stands pleasantly, on the south side of the river,

[1] " Woodford House, which is half a mile north of Newtown-
Gore, is built on the ruins of another of the O'Rorke's Castles.
The estate was formerly well wooded, and remarkable for its
oaks, and there are still two fine walled gardens of considerable
extent.   It was a place of great splendour, and belonged to the
ancestors of W. Ormsby-Gore, Esq., of Porkington, Shropshire."—Lewis's *Topog. Dict., Ireland*, 1837.

[2] M.P. for Co. Leitrim, 1729 (in place of his father), till 1760,
again, 1769 ; *m.*, 1733, Sarah, youngest sister of John Bligh,
created Earl of Darnley, and had issue, William, who *d.* an in-
fant.   He *d.* 1769, and was succeeded by his nephew, William
Gore, in his estates and the representation of the county, ancestor of the Ormsby-Gores, of Porkington, Shropshire, now
Barons Harlech.

Sir Arthur Gore, first Bart. of Newtown-Gore, Co. Mayo
(second son of Sir Paul Gore, first Bart. of Manor Gore), left
issue, three sons, the second of whom, William Gore, of Woodford, M.P. for Co. Leitrim, 1703, till his death, January, 1729,
and *Custos Rotulorum, m.*, 1696, Catherine (*d.* 1747), daughter
of Sir Robert Newcomen, Bart., and had issue, two sons; 1. Wm.,
his successor abovenamed; 2. Robert, *m.* Letitia, daughter of
Henry Brooke, Esq., of Colebrooke, Fermanagh, M.P., and had
issue, William, who succeeded his uncle as above.

in a small lawn, encompassed with large woods, through
which is cut a grand avenue leading to the house, and
several other pleasing walks and vistas. The basins
and large canals formed by the river, the woods and
lawns interspersed, present the eye with an inchanting
prospect ; to make it the more entertaining, the whole
is a deer-park, and this curious gentleman has, at a
great expense, made a large collection of the rarest
foreign birds and beasts, both wild and tame. The
river, a little below this seat, enters into the County of
Cavan, and, in a course of six miles, reaches the small
market-town of Ballyconnell, where is a redoubt.

Here, on the south side of the river, defended by
huge old trees, stands a beautiful new seat[1] of the Rev.
George Leslie, son to the Rev. Dr. Leslie,[2] who was so

---

[1] " Ballyconnell House, the residence of John Enery, Esq.,
is beautifully situated in a fine demesne, on the Woodford river,
which winds through the extensive and well-wooded grounds
in its course to Lake Annagh, and Lough Erne. The house
was erected, in 1764, by the late George Montgomery, Esq., on
the site of the castle of Ballyconnell, which was entirely
destroyed by an accidental fire. There is a chalybeate spring
in the demesne."—Lewis's *Topog. Dict., Ireland*, 1837.

[2] John Leslie D.D. (son of James Leslie, by Catherine, fourth
daughter of Alex. Conyngham, of Mount Charles, Dean of
Raphoe), Rector of Derryvollan, Co. Fermanagh, when attainted
1689, subsequently held the livings of Donaghmore and of
Urney. He raised a company of foot, and a troop of dragoons ;
at the head of the latter he performed important services. He
possessed large estates, considerably augmented by grants of
forfeitures, particularly, in 1700, of Tarbert, Co. Kerry. He
d., of asthma, 1700, leaving issue, by Mariana, his wife,
daughter of Rev. Humphrey Galbraith (by Isabel, fourth
daughter of Sir Paul Gore, first Bart. of Magherebeg, or Manor
Gore), with five daughters [of whom Letitia, or Lettice (Will
proved, 1767), m. Walter Johnston, Esq., of Kilmore, Co.
Fermanagh (d. ante 1729), and had issue—1. Francis, of Kilmore, d. s. p. 1740 ; 1. Mariana, m. John Sinclair, Esq., of
Holly Hill, Co. Tyrone ; 2. Jane ; 3. Mary], three sons—1. John

greatly distinguished, by his valour and conduct, among
the Inniskilleners. This seat is of hewn stone without,
and elegantly finished with stucco work within. The
front is diversified with dark and light-coloured stones,
resembling a pavement : it looks to the west ; and the
river answers to it as a canal ; at its north end it
breaks into a cascade, and, twisting round to the east
side, it sports in a deep serpentine channel through
several large plantations and woods, and mixes with
some large lakes that lie behind them ; thence continuing its serpentine course for six miles further, it enters
Lough Erne. The whole course of this river is about
twenty miles through a gravelly, dry country ; notwith-
standing which its channels are deep, and its streams
slow and silent. A little pains would make it navigable
through most of its course.

Leslie, *unmarried*, killed at Aughrim, 12 July, 1691 ; 2. James
Leslie inherited Tarbert, &c., Co. Kerry, *d. circa* 1724, leaving
issue by Sarah, his wife—John, James, George, Sarah ; 3.
George Leslie, D.D., successively Rector of Clones and of Kilmore, *m.* 1711, Margaret, daughter of Major John Montgomery
(and sister of Col. Alex. Montgomery, Scots' Greys, of Convoy
House, Co. Donegal, M.P., who *d. s. p.*, and bequeathed to his
sister, and her son George Leslie, the Ballyconnell estate, which
he had purchased, 1724, for £8,000, from the Executors of
Humphrey Guyllym, son (?) of Major Meredith Guilliams, of
Ballyconnell, in 1692), and *d.* 1754, leaving issue with two
daughters (Margaret Leslie, *d. unm.*, and Catherine, *m.*——
Hamilton, and had issue—Sir John Charles Hamilton, Bart.,
m.——, and had a son, John *d. s. p.*, and a daughter, Margaret,
m. 1762, John Enery, of whom hereafter), two sons—James
Leslie, D.D., Prebendary of Durham ; and George Leslie, who
assumed the name and arms of Montgomery, was M.P. for
Strabane, 1764-1768 ; Cavan Co., 1769, till his death in 1787,
m., 1752, Hannah (*d.* at Bath, Jan., 1786), second daughter of
Right Hon. Nat. Clements, M.P. (p. 2), and had issue one son,
George (a lunatic), *d. s. p.* 20 March, 1841, *æt.* 87, and four
daughters (of whom—3. Mary, and 4. Nathalina, *d. unm.*, and)—
1. Hannah, *m.* Rev. Joseph Story ; and, 2. Alicia, *m.*, his first
wife, 1791, her cousin, Nat. Sneyd, Esq., of Dublin, and Bally-

LOUGH ERNE.

The place where it (the river of Aughalane) enters
Lough Erne is a wide, flat corkous[1] meadow called " The
Bloody Pass," from an engagement that happened there
in summer, 1689, between a small party of Inniskilleners and a detachment of King James's army,
whom the former routed in attempting the pass, either
killing or drowning most of them in the river.

COMBER WATER.

About a mile lower on the east side enters into
Lough Erne the river of Castle Saunderson—called
Comber Water—which is as large, or rather larger, than

connell (son of Edward Sneyd, Esq., M.P., Carrick, 1777-1781,
and his wife, Hannah Honora, only daughter of James
King, Esq., of Gola Abbey, Co. Fermanagh), M.P., Carrick,
1795-1799 ; Co. Cavan, 1800-1826, and *Custos Rotulorum*, and
she *d. s. p.* 1793. Mr. Sneyd *m.*, secondly, 1806, Anne Burgh,
sister of second Lord Downes, and *d. s. p.* 1833, having been
shot in Westmoreland Street, Dublin, by Mr. John Mason, a
lunatic.

The above-named John Enery left issue, by Margaret Hamil-
ton, a son, John Enery, Lieut.-Col., Kilkenny Militia, who
claimed and succeeded to Ballyconnell, *m.* Sarah Ainsworth
Blunt, of Kilkenny, and had issue—1. George, *d. unm.* ; 2.
Joseph, *d. unm.* ; 3. William Hamilton Enery (*d.* 1854), of
Ballyconnell House, D.L., *m.* Alicia, daughter of Brooke Taylor
Ottley, Esq., and left issue a daughter, Constance Isabella, *m.*,
1864, Capt. Stuart Davis Cartwright, who assumed the name of
Enery ; 4. John. (Partly from *Hist. of Montgomery of Bally-
leck, &c.*, by Lieut.-Gen. George S. Montgomery, C.S.I.)

Samuel Black Roe, Esq., C.B., Deputy-Surgeon-General in the
army, of Ballyconnell, eldest son of late George Roe, M.D. (by
Eliza, daughter of late Major Samuel Noble, H.E.I.C.S.), succeeded
to Ballyconnell, on the death of his mother, in 1876.—Walford's
County Families, 1889.

[1] " Corcach, corcas, a marsh, low, swampy ground."—Joyce's
Irish Names of Places, 1869.

the former (river of Aughalane). It rises in the southern
part of the County Monaghan, and, by its various
branches and large lakes, wherewith it mixes, it waters
the greater part of that county. It passes through
Clones,[1] a market-town on the borders of Fermanagh
and Monaghan, and thence, in a course of six miles, it
bends broad and deep under Castle Saunderson.[2]

The situation of this seat is chosen with both spirit
and taste; it stands on the top of a hill, which commands all around, and rises high over the south side of

[1] "Clownish" in MS. "Cluan Innis," Island of Retreat.
(Lewis.)

[2] It was burnt by King James's troops, under Galmoy, in 1689,
and its then owner was attainted. He was Robert Saunderson
[eldest son of Col. Robert Saunderson, who served with great
distinction under Gustavus Adolphus, and settling at Castle
Saunderson, died there in 1676, leaving issue—1. Robert, second
of Castle Saunderson; 2. James, of Drumkeen, Co. Cavan, m.
Anne Whyte, of Redhills, and had issue—Alexander, who
succeeded his uncle Robert, and James, of Drumcassidy, or
Cloverhill, collateral ancestor of the present Samuel Sanderson,
Esq., D.L., of that seat (p. 3); 3. William, of Co. Westmeath],
Colonel of a Regiment under King William III., M.P. for the
Co., and d. s. p. 1723, leaving his estates to his nephew, Alex-
ander, who m. his cousin Mabella, daughter of William Saunder-
son, of Westmeath, aforenamed, and was ancestor of the present
Lieut.-Col. Edward James Saunderson, of Castle Saunderson,
D.L., Member of Parliament for North Armagh (for Co. Cavan,
1865-1874).

The family claims the Viscounty of Castleton, in the Irish
Peerage, conferred, 1592, on Sir Nicholas Saunderson, of Saxby,
Co. Lincoln; and a proffered Barony of Castleton was, it is
said, refused by its representative at the time of the Union.—
Burke's *Landed Gentry.*

"Nearly adjoining the demesne of Farnham is Castle Saunderson, the seat of A. Saunderson, Esq., surrounded by a
luxuriant demesne commanding the most beautiful views of
Lough Erne.

"Clover Hill, an excellent mansion, the seat of J. Sanderson,
Esq., has also a very beautiful demesne richly adorned, and
bordered by a spacious lake."—Lewis's *Topog. Dict., Ireland,*
1837.

the river ; at the bottom of the hill are some plantations ; and, from the castle to the skirts all around, the hill descends in a verdant, spacious lawn—here and there interspersed with single large forest trees. The boldness of its aspect makes it naturally a stronghold, and gives it an uncommon air of grandeur ; it looks majestically over the river to the north, and a great part of Lough Erne to the west.

This river is navigable for large boats up to Clones.

It and the former river of Aughalane are the southern bounds that separate Fermanagh from Cavan. A little below its opening into the Lough is a large island that stretches a mile.

In no part of Ireland, except on the plains of Aughrim, was so great a slaughter made of the native Irish in the last wars as in this river and the country which lies between it and Newtownbutler—a village standing three miles northwards. As this extraordinary battle has been mentioned only in general by historians, I hope it will be no unacceptable digression to relate it more particularly, as I have it from the mouths of persons of undoubted veracity, who were present at it, and are yet alive.

In July, 1689, a numerous and well-appointed army was led down from Munster, under the conduct of the Lords Galmoy[1] and Mountcashell. They encamped at

[1] General Piers Butler, third Viscount Galmoy. The Rev. Dr. Hughes, in his *Church of S. Werburgh, Dublin*, 1889, prints a curious letter from Francis Marsh, D.D., Archbishop of Dublin, dated "S. Sepulchre's, Jan. 31, 1685-6," to his Chancellor, William King, subsequently Bishop of Derry and Archbishop of Dublin, relating to some offence committed by Lord Galmoy :—

"My Ld. Gilmoy was wᵗʰ me, and earnestly desires, as I doe, that to-morrow being a church day, you would be pleased

Belturbet, where, being joined by the northern Irish,
under the command of Cohanaughmore-Macguire,[1] they
formed a regular army of 7,000 men.   In order utterly
to extirpate the Inniskilliners, a plan was laid for their
being attacked at once by three armies from different
quarters—by Sarsfield,[2] with a Connaught army from
the west ; by the Duke of Berwick,[3] who covered the
Siege of Derry, from the north ; and by this Munster
army from the south ; so that this handful of men
seemed, in the eyes of their enemies, to be encompassed
in a net, out of which they could not escape.   But,
happy for them, they knew not their danger.   The rout
of the Connaught army by Colonel Lloyd[4] at the head
of 1,000 Inniskilleners has been already related.   The

to appoint a vestry in yᵉ afternoon, when upon notice to me he
will attend you, acknowledg his errour, and bestow his charity
upon yᵉ poore of yᵉ parish, which I pray you to accept.   This
is only upon his own accᵗ.   I desire you will signify to me the
time.   It is expedient to be done before my Ld. Lt. arrives.

" I am Sʳ,
" Most affectionately yʳ friend and servᵗ.,
" franc. Dublin."

This act of church discipline is said to have been carried out.

[1] Colonel of King James's 43rd Regiment, Sheriff of Fermanagh, 1687, 1688, and sometime Governor of the same
county.   He fell at Aughrim, 23rd July, 1691.

[2] Patrick Sarsfield, created by James II., Earl of Lucan, and
a Major-General.   Killed at Battle of Landen, 1693 ; *m.* Lady
Honora De Burgh, and had a son who *d. s. p.* in Flanders.

[3] James FitzJames, a natural son of James II. (by Arabella
Churchill, sister of the great Duke of Marlborough), a Marshal
of France, one of the greatest generals of his time ; slain at
Philipsburgh, 1734 ; *m.*, 1695, Lady Honora Sarsfield, widow
of the preceding, and left issue by her (who died 1698).

[4] Thomas Lloyd (eldest son of Captain Owen Lloyd, of an
ancient Welsh family, who acquired estates in the Co. Roscommon) came to Enniskillen in January, 1689, and was chosen

attack of the Duke of Berwick shall be spoken of when
I come to the spot where the action happened. My
business now is to give some account of the Munster
army.

The very day that Colonel Lloyd returned from the
slaughter of the Connaught army, an express arrived in
Enniskillen, by water, from Colonel Creichton, to inform
them that he and his two companies were closely besieged in his Castle of Crum by the Munster army, and
requiring their immediate assistance. Next morning,
in order to reach this place betimes, which is sixteen
miles from Enniskillen, the whole body of the Inniskilleners, amounting to 1,500 men, set out before sun-
rise, leaving few, except the women, to guard the town.
The main body marched by the great road through
Maguire's-bridge; but a small party, consisting of two
troops of horse and two companies of foot, led on by the
gallant Martin Armstrong,[1] took a shorter road, near

by the Inniskilleners to be their commander in the field.
"Under whose conduct," writes MacCarmick in *Farther Impartial Account of the Actions of the Inniskilling Men*, "we
never failed accomplishing what we designed, but without him
could not, or never did anything." He was a colonel in the
army, and died *s. p.*

[1] Captain Armstrong, of Longfield, Co. Leitrim, descended,
like the Dunbars, Grahams, Johnstons, &c., in Fermanagh,
from a warlike border clan, whence sprang Andrew Armstrong,
who, in the seventeenth century, crossed over into Ulster, and,
settling in Fermanagh, *m.*, as his second wife, Elizabeth,
daughter of Martin Johnston (*vivens*, 1642), and *d.* 1671, *æt.* 95,
leaving a numerous posterity, now represented by the Baronets
(created 1841) of Gallen, King's Co.

"About two and a-half miles to the south (of Newtown-Gore)
are the ruins of the Castle of Longfield, which, from the gable
that still remains, appears to have been of strong but rude
masonry. It was taken possession of by Major Martin Armstrong after the battle of Cavan."—Lewis's *Topog. Dict., Ireland*, 1837.

the Lough side, by Lisnaskea. Here, in a close lane,
they met, in full march, Lord Clare's[1] regiment of
dragoons, which were the flower of King James's army.
These were commanded by Sir James Cotter,[2] whom
King James had, from a trooper in the Guards, raised
to a lieutenant-colonel's commission, the honour of
knighthood, and an estate in the County of Cork, for
his assassinating Lord Lisle[3] as he came out of a church
in Switzerland. Armstrong quickly lined the hedges
with the foot, and then, making a feint to attack with
his troopers, retired as if in disorder, till he drew the
enemy into ambush ; the foot at once making an unex-
pected fire, caused a great slaughter ; the horse at the
same instant facing about, and falling on them with
incredible fury, made such havoc that of this brave regiment very few escaped. The terror and swiftness

[1] Daniel O'Brien, third Viscount Clare, raised in the Co.
Clare two regiments of infantry, and one of dragoons, distinguished in Irish tradition as " the dragoon bue," or yellow
dragoons, for the service of James II., which he commanded at
the Boyne. He was outlawed 1691, and *d.* soon after.

[2] In *Notes and Queries*, June 1, 1889, appears an interesting
article questioning Sir James Cotter's participation in this
crime. His son was executed, 1720, for his devotion to the
House of Stuart, and his grandson was created a Baronet in
1763.

[3] John Lisle, (*jure uxoris*) of Moyles Court, Hants one of
Bradshaw's two assistants at the trial of Charles I., and one of
Cromwell's peers, escaped on the Restoration to Switzerland,
and was assassinated either at Lausanne or Vevay, 1667, at the
instigation, according to some, of Queen Henrietta Maria. His
widow, the Lady Alicia, daughter and heir of Sir White
Becensaw, Knt., of Moyles Court, was arbitrarily tried by
the infamous Jeffreys, and beheaded at Winchester, 2nd Sep-
tember, 1685, *æt.* 80. His posterity is extinct, and his eldest
brother's line terminated in co-heiresses, one of whom is represented by the family of Phillipps, of Garendon Park and Grace
Dieu Manor, Co. Leicester.—Burke's *Landed Gentry.*

wherewith they fled gave rise to that irony among the Munster Irish, which remains to this day—" Coss! coss! a Dragoon buoy!" that is, " Stop! stop! the yellow Dragoon!"—the livery of Clare's regiment being scarlet, faced with yellow. While the fugitives, flying back to the main army, struck an universal panic through it. The Inniskilleners, animated with this success, and led on by those stout men, whose names ought ever to be remembered—Tiffin,[1] Creichton, Lloyd, Carleton[2]—quickened their march for four miles farther, to the village of Newtownbutler, that stands a mile south-east from Crum Castle. Being arrived there, they found the Irish army drawn up in order of battle on the south side of the town, upon a rising hill, surrounded with a large, deep red bog, through which there was no pass to the hill but by a narrow causeway. This was defended by six field pieces, planted over it on the ascent of the hill. By this situation they seemed to be as secure as in a strong camp, and, so far from needing to fear an attack from an handful of men, that they might have sustained one from an army ten times as numerous as themselves.

[1] " Tiphany " in MS.—Zechariah Tiffin was Major in Queen's Foot Regiment in 1687 ; Colonel, 26th June, 1689, Inniskilling Foot, till 1702; Brigadier-General, 1698 ; probably died before 1706, as there is a petition from Margaret Tiffin, *widow*, mentioned that year in *Despatches from Lord Justices of Ireland, 1706-1712.* Add. MSS., 9,717 B.M.

[2] Captain Christopher Carleton, (*jure uxoris*) of Tullymargie Castle (of an ancient Cumberland family), *m.* Anne, daughter of George Hamilton, Esq., of Tullymargie Castle, Fermanagh (her will, made 29th April, 1722, was proved 9th October, 1729), and died, leaving issue (his will made 18th April, 1716, was proved 9th May, 1717) : 1. Alexander of Tullymargie ; 2. George ; 3. Lancelot ; 1. Anne, *m.* Robert Weir.

Accordingly, Colonel Tiffin, who was an old, expe-
rienced officer, observing this strong situation of the
enemy, thought the attacking them a rash attempt;
but since, after advancing so far, it was unavoidable, he
was for going the surer way to work by leading on the
Inniskilleners in regular columns; but Lloyd, who had
but a few days before observed the effect of their impe-
tuous courage—too great to be restrained within military
rules—advised to let them proceed in their own way,
whereupon they, scarce staying for their commanders,
darted like lightning through all parts of the bog,
attacked the enemy on the face of the hill, sword in
hand, in a few minutes drove them from their field-
pieces, which commanded the pass, and, by turning
them on the enemy, at once made a slaughter among
them, and left the pass of the causeway open for their
own horse. Here, at the first onset, Captain Cooper
took prisoner the General Justin Macarthy, Lord Viscount Mountcashell, while he was in vain endeavouring
by his own example to animate his cowardly troops.
He was esteemed by far the best and most worthy of
King James's generals. The confusion, heightened by
the turning of the great guns and the General's cap-
tivity, struck an universal panic, and the rout soon
became general; they fled through bogs and fastnesses,
for three miles, to the river of Castle Saunderson, the
Inniskilleners, and the two companies which had been
besieged in Crum Castle, making all the way horrible
slaughter. A party of horse, getting before the flying
enemy, seized Watling Bridge, the only pass over the
river. Being thus hemmed in, and not knowing
whither to flee, they, in their fear—which always sug-
gests the worst counsels—drew up on a nook of the

river where it is very deep, just under Castle Saunderson. Here they stood to their arms, not having the
wisdom to ask quarter, nor the courage to fight. In
this fatal spot the whole brigade, consisting of near
4,000 men, were driven into the river and perished, not
one man escaping; so that, reckoning those who were
lost here, in the chase, in the battle, and in the defeat
of Clare's Regiment, it has been computed that of this
army a full half perished that day; the remaining,
making up the river towards Clones, found a way to
escape.

The Inniskilleners, in this battle, carried their resent-
ment possibly beyond the just bounds, being greatly
provoked to it, by the ignominious treatment and the
inhuman murder of the Dean of Kilmore's son and
Lieut. Carleton, who were dear to them, and whom
Lord Galmoy had hanged at Belturbet a few days
before. That perfidious lord was well-nigh giving
Colonel Creichton the same fate: having drawn him to
an interview on the public faith, he had him arrested
because he would not deliver up his Castle of Crum,
and would have put him to death had not Lord Mountcashell, enraged at such perfidious dealings, torn him
out of his hands by force, and conducted him safe home
to his castle. Nor did Lord Mountcashell lose his
reward for this instance of justice and honour; his life
was spared in the hottest part of the battle; he was
conducted to Enniskillen, together with 400 prisoners
more, many of whom were spared on his account. He
was there allowed the liberty of the town on his parole.
After some time, finding there was little prospect of
his ransom, he caused artfully a rumour to be raised
that he intended to escape, whereupon the Governour

clapt a guard on him, by this act releasing him from
his parole. The guard, observing the freedom which
he before was indulged in, were remiss, and the Ser-
geant Atcheson, being bribed, carried him off at night
by water, for which act he was shot the next day. Lord
Mountcashell, escaping into France, was tried for the
breach of his parole by a Court of Honour, and, making
the circumstances of his escape appear, was acquitted.[1]

This victory[2] contributed to the raising the siege of
Derry with precipitation, the Irish army there dreading
that the Inniskilleners might cut off their retreat.

If this digression from the thread of these hints be
too long, I hope it may be pardoned in a person who,
being placed by Providence among this gallant people,
was desirous to preserve these particulars, which—if left
only to tradition—would probably, in another genera-
tion, be lost.

Lough Erne.

Two miles northward from the mouth of Castle
Saunderson River, on the east side of the lake, stands
Crum Castle,[3] the seat of Abraham Creichton,[4] Esq.

[1] He had been created Viscount Mountcashell in 1689. In
the battle of Newtownbutler his horse was shot under him, and
he would have been slain "but for the goodness of his armour."
One shot " would certainly have killed him had it not been for
his watch, which the bullet beat all to pieces "—(MacCarmick).
After his escape to France, he commanded in Catalonia, and on
the Rhine, where he was wounded. He died, s. p., 1694.

[2] The Inniskilleners lost but two of their officers, Capt. Robert
Corry, and Cornet William Bell, with not half a score private
men, and very few wounded.

[3] The ruins of this old castle, heavily clothed with ivy, present
a beautifully picturesque appearance, and the famous yew tree
still flourishes. " The only seat of importance (in the parish of

It is built on a flat piece of ground commanded by hills
that are covered with thick woods, and stands so close
on the shore that, in winter, the waves dash violently
against it. Its walls are strong, but it has no outer
wall, nor can it hold long out against a well-appointed
force, by reason of the hills which mount so high above
it, within musket shot, yet the courage of the owner
and his tenants was such that they held out against a

Galloon)—the residence of the Earl of Erne, about three miles
from Newtown Butler—a handsome mansion recently erected—
in which is still preserved the armour worn by M'Carthy More
at the battle of Kilgarret."—Lewis's *Topog. Dict., Ireland,*
1837.

[4] Sheriff of Fermanagh, 1673 ; M.P. for same Co., 1692, and for
Enniskillen, 1695-99 (son of John Crichton, Esq., by Mary Irvine,
of the Castle Irvine family). He raised a regiment of foot,
named after its Colonel, "Creighton's Foot" (*v.* Appendix II.),
and commanded it at Aughrim. He was attainted in 1689. He
m. Mary, daughter of James Spottiswoode, Bishop of Clogher,
and *d.* 1705, having had issue—I. Captain James Crichton, who
d. 1701, leaving, by Hester Willoughby, his wife, issue—1.
John, of Crum, who *d. unm.,* 1715-16, bequeathing his estates
to his uncle, Brigadier David Crichton, of Lifford, and his
heirs male; 2. Mary; 3. Sidney, Mrs. Eccles—II. David Crichton,
at the age of 18, the gallant defender of Crum, in 1689 ; Captain
in his father's Regiment till 1698 ; Major in Lord of Ikerin's
foot, 1703-4 ; and attained the rank of Major-General ; M.P.
for Augher, 1695-99, and for Lifford (the family borough until
the Union), 1703, 1713, 1715, and 1727, till his death ; Governor
of the Royal Hospital, Kilmainham. He *m.,* 1700, Catherine
(*d.* 1759), daughter of Richard Southwell, and sister of first
Baron Southwell, of Castle Matrix, and died 1728 (buried,
3 June, at St. Andrew's, Dublin), leaving, with daughters, a son,
Abraham, born 1703, created, 1768, Baron Erne, of Crum Castle,
in the peerage of Ireland, whose son, the second Baron, was
advanced to the dignities of Viscount (1781), and Earl (1789).
The third, and late, Earl, Sir John Crichton, K.P., Lieutenant,
and *Custos Rotulorum,* of the Co., was created, 13 Jan., 1876,
Baron Fermanagh, of Lisnaskea, in the peerage of the United
Kingdom, and his son, the present, and fourth, Earl, succeeded
him in the Lieutenancy of the Co.

The family claims descent from a branch of the ancient house
of Frendraught, Aberdeenshire.

small siege till relieved. There are still to be seen the
marks of several cannon-balls shot at it, which only
struck off some splinters from the stones, but made no
farther impression. The besieged found great advantage from the long fowling-pieces, with double rests,
used along this lake—with one of these they had nigh
killed the Lord Galmoy; he came to reconnoitre the
castle from an hill near an English mile distant—where
he thought himself secure, knowing that the besieged had
no great guns. While he stood at this distance, with a
glass in his hand to drink confusion to the rebels of
Crum, as he termed them, an expert fowler, from the
battlements of the castle, levelling one of these long
guns at the crowd, broke the glass in his hand, and
killed the man who stood next; this deterred the
besiegers from making too near approaches.

Frontward, from the castle towards the south, a
pleasant garden stretches along the side of the lake. In
the centre of this garden stands a curious yew tree,
planted about seventy years ago ; its straight stem
ascends about ten feet, thence, shooting out its branches
horizontally, it forms a circular shade about seventy-
five feet in circumference, which is supported by three
circles of wooden pillars, from which, to the stem, there
is continued a strong range of rafters that bear up its
weighty branches from the circumference ; the venerable head of the tree ascends regularly in a thickly
woven, low cone, and forms a shade impenetrable by
the heaviest rain.

Lough Erne, which for the space of six miles from
Belturbet to this place, observes the form of a large,
silent, beautiful river, just at this castle opens into
several wide, extended bays, some of which are two

miles in length. These are all encompassed with
pleasant hills, or islands that rise gently in small hills
from the water, all of them clothed with woods, some
of which are large oak woods. The exquisite interspersion of water, hills, islands, woods, and lawns,
form here a landscape which is more agreeable than
the fancy can well conceive without seeing it.[1] It
is usual for gentlemen sailing by this place to dis-
charge some guns in compliment to the venerable
castle. Some seconds after the noise of the shot has
seemingly quite ceased, the echo begins, which is
repeated in loud peals from the several bays successively, till at last the very echo of the echo dies away
like the noise of thunder at a great distance.[2]

The lake continues to spread much in this form for
the space of seven miles, from Crum to Knockninny.
In all this space it is interspersed with a variety of
pleasant islands, of an hilly form, covered with wood.

[1] Sir John Davis was not slow in recognising the natural
beauties and advantages of Fermanagh. When writing to
Salisbury from Enniskillen, in the autumn of 1609, he says :—
" We have now finished our service in Fermanagh, which is so
pleasant and fruitful a country that if I should make a full
description thereof, it would rather be taken for a poetical fic-
tion than a true and serious narration. The fresh lake called
Lough Erne—being more than forty miles in length, and
abounding in fresh water fish of all kinds, and containing one
hundred dispersed islands—divides that country into two parts.
The land on either side of the lough, rising in little hills of
eighty or a hundred acres apiece, is the fattest and richest soil
in all Ulster."
Besides the inhabited islands and those available for agricul-
tural and pastoral purposes, there are many smaller ones ; the
total number has been computed at over three hundred.

[2] Not far from Crum the lake winds round the island of
Innisrath, the picturesque residence of the Hon. Mrs. H.
Cavendish Butler (Lady Emerson Tennant), and passes Ross-
ferry, that of Lieut. Gartside Tipping, R.N.

The islands are so agreeably scattered that they form a
succession of large basins into which, when a boat is
entered, it seems to be land-locked, so that, unless to
those who are acquainted with the land-marks, it is not
easy to find the outlet from one of these basins to the
next, and the eye of the passenger is so entertained
with nature in her beauty, that it forsakes the prospect
with pain.

From one of the most spacious of these basins opens
to the passenger Manor Waterhouse, the seat of the
Rev. Dr. Samuel Madden.[1] It is agreeably situated on
the eastern side of the Lough, at the distance of a

[1] John Madden, of Enfield, Middlesex (grandson of John
Madden, of Bloxham Beauchamp, Oxon., Esq.), *m.*, 1635,
Elizabeth (died 1671), eldest daughter, and, in her issue, heiress
of Charles Waterhouse, Esq., of Castle, or Manor, Water-
house, and *d.* 1661, *æt.* 63. His son, John Madden, M.D., of
Manor Waterhouse, born 1648, *m.*, 1680, his first wife, Mary,
daughter of Samuel Molyneux, Esq., of Castle Dillon, Co.
Armagh, and *d.* 1703, leaving by her Samuel Madden, born
1686; D.D., T.C.D., 1723 ; Rector of Newtownbutler; one of the
founders, in 1740, of the Royal Dublin Society, first named
" The Society of Arts ; " a great benefactor to his country.
" His was a name Ireland ought to honour," said Dr. Samuel
Johnson. He projected, 1731, a scheme for promoting learn-
ing in Trinity College, Dublin, by premiums to the best
answerers at the quarterly examinations, and, by a codicil to
his will, left large bequests to the same University. In 1740,
he settled £100 per annum to be distributed as premiums by
the Royal Dublin Society for useful inventions, sculpture, and
painting, whence he is known in his family as " Premium
Madden." He was sometime tutor to Frederick, Prince of
Wales, and author of *Memoirs of the Twentieth Century, being
Original Letters of State under George the Sixth, received and
revealed in the year 1728.* In six vols., 1733. One thousand
copies of Vol. I. of this work were printed, but, in less than a
fortnight, 900 copies were delivered up to the author, and, for
political reasons, probably destroyed. His *Reflections and Resolutions Proper for the Gentlemen of Ireland,* &c., 1738, became
so rare that it was re-printed at the expense of Mr. Thomas
Pleasants, of Dublin, in 1816. He also compiled genealogical
collections, and a *History of the Co. Fermanagh,* written in

short mile, yet, as the ground agreeably ascends the
whole way, it appears just to hang over it.   The house[1]
stands on the ridge of one of those hills that resemble
a ship with the keel turned up.   It is placed at the
western end of the hill, as on the stern end of the keel,
and the avenue from the front—which looks eastward—
is carried along the keel towards the bows.   The approach of the house is towards the eastern front, to
which the entrance is through a large pleasure garden,
that contains a variety of gravel walks, wall fruits, ever-
greens, and a curious collection of flowers and shrubs.
From this there is an ascent, by several steps, into a

1718 and 1719 (Appendix III.), which MSS., at one time in the
possession of the late Ulster, Sir William Betham, were, after
his death, purchased, in 1860, by the late Sir Thomas Phillipps,
Bart., for his great collection at Thirlestane House Library,
Cheltenham.   Dr. Madden m. Jane, daughter of Captain Hugh
Magill, of Kirkstown, Co. Down (by Lucy, daughter and eventual heiress of Charles Balfour, Esq., of Castle Balfour (p. 41),
and died 1765.   He had issue two sons and five daughters ; 1.
Samuel Molyneux Madden, Sheriff, Fermanagh, 1749, $d.\,s.\,p.\,v.$
1784 ; 2. John Madden, of Maddenton, now Hilton, Co. Mon-
aghan, and Manor Waterhouse, m., 1752, Anne, daughter of
Robert Cope, Esq., of Loughall, M.P., and was ancestor of the
present John Madden, Esq., D.L., of Hilton Park and Manor·
Waterhouse, and of John Madden, Esq., D.L., of Rosle
Manor, Co· Fermanagh ; 1. Lucy, m. Alexander Sanderson, of
Clover Hill (p. 26), and had issue ; 2. Elizabeth, m., 1761, John
Hawkshaw ; 3. Jane, d. unm. ; 4. Alice, d. unm. ; 5. Mary,
d. unm.
   Sir Edward Waterhouse, of Castle Waterhouse, M.P. for
Carrickfergus, 1585 ; Chancellor, Irish Exchequer, $d.\,s.\,p.$ 1591.
Charles Waterhouse, of the same seat, an undertaker of 1,000
acres in B. Clankelly, m. Ethelred (d. 1640), sister of Sir
Stephen Butler, Knt. (p. 20), and, dying 1638, left issue, with
Mrs. Madden, a son, Charles, m., 1634, Elizabeth Cope, and
had four sons, who d. unm., and a daughter, Anne, m. Patrick
Harrison, and had issue a son, Charles.

[1] The old castle had been burnt down by the Irish army
before the Battle of Newtownbutler, 31st July, 1689, and was
only partially restored.

hall twenty-four feet square, wainscotted and curiously
carved ; in this a beautiful gallery for music. From
the hall is continued a great parlour of the like dimensions, which, through a long avenue, affords a prospect
that terminates in a broad basin of Lough Erne. This
room and the hall are almost covered with fine pieces
of painting, several of which are originals, done by the
names that have been most famous over Europe. On
each hand of the hall, and from the parlour, go off
large apartments. Over the doors which lead into the
house are engraved sentences out of the classics, express-
ing the beauty and agreeableness of the country and
fine situation, and, indeed, the whole seems to be
finished with a classical taste and elegance. On the
south side of the house are large gardens, with several
walks and terraces that descend steeply to a deep,
solemn glen, through which runs a large rivulet, which,
in some places, murmurs gently, in others roars,
through the hollowest part of the glen, by the several
artificial cascades over which it pours. The north side
of the hill, which descends from the house, is covered
with a thick, young wood, which is cut out into an
infinite number of shady walks, terraces, recesses, and
labyrinths. At the bottom of this wilderness winds a
rivulet as large as the former, in a great number of
meanders, sometimes gliding in a deep, clear channel,
again breaking in cascades ; all along its bank is a
small, serpentine gravel walk, which attends all its
twistings through the wilderness which make up an
English mile. Along this walk are, here and there,
pleasant bowers interwoven of branches of trees and
flowering shrubs, which hang over the brook ; the
banks are diversified with a variety of flowers, succeed-

ing one another through the seasons ; in several places there opens into this walk little winding alleys, which lead into the darkest parts of the wilderness, and generally terminate in something agreeable ; one of these winds into a circle, in the centre of which is piled up a pyramid of bones, and round the circumference are erected tombstones with curious inscriptions. Throughout all the wilderness nature appears in her native beauty and charming wildness ; the strokes of art are scattered with so loose and easy an hand as serve only to display nature the more, while they are scarce perceived themselves. The whole seat seems a fit retreat for the Muses, and it is but a just compliment to the numerous, agreeable family that inhabit it, to say it is not without the Graces !

Two small miles northward stands, near the lough, the market town of Lisnaskea,[1] and at the south of the town Castle Balfour, the seat of Harry Balfour,[2] Esq.

[1] " A tolerably strong castle belonging to Charles Belfore, Esq. . . . . Ere Galmoy came (in March, 1689) the length of Lisnaskey, a cursed fellow, one Kemp, with some of the rabble of the country his consorts, burnt that pretty village, to the great loss of the inhabitants and the worthy gentleman that owned it, as also a prejudice to Iniskilling, it being capable of quartering above a regiment of men. . . . . But ere the town was burnt, we had brought from thence a many tuns of iron belonging to Mr. Belfore, and most of the lead of his house, which proved very serviceable to us, both to horse and foot."— (MacCarmick.)

The Castle Balfour estate passed by purchase to the Earls of Erne.

[2] Eldest son of Blayney Townley, Esq., of Co. Louth, by Lucy (widow successively of Hugh Magill, of Kirkstown, Co. Down, p. 39, and of Col. Robert Johnston), daughter and eventual heiress of Charles Balfour, Esq., of Castle Balfour (attainted, 1689), son of Sir Wm. Balfour, who acquired the Fermanagh estates of his kinsman, Sir James Balfour, Lord Clanawley. Mr. Harry Townley succeeded to Castle Balfour on the death,

It is a large old castle, encompassed with groves and plantations. By the several improvements and ornaments added to it by the present owner, it makes a shining figure from the lake all along the country lying on the opposite western side of the lake.

Opposite to this place Lough Erne spreads wide, near four miles in breadth, having, to the south side, hanging over it the pleasant hill of Knockninny,[1] and on the west the low ground and bogs of Glenawly, from which the country ascends coarse till it rises to the high mountains over which stands exalted Cuilcagh.[2]

1739, *s. p.*, of his maternal uncle, Wm. Balfour, M.P., Augher B. (who had been attainted, 1689), and assumed the surname of Balfour. He *m.* Anne Percy (admin. 1741), and had issue (with a daughter, Emilia) a son, Wm. Charles, who *d. s. p.*, and the estate reverted to his (Harry Balfour's) next brother, Blayney Townley, who also assumed the surname of Balfour, and was ancestor of the present Blayney Reynell Townley Balfour, Esq., D.L., of Townley Hall, Co. Louth.

[1] On the north side of the lough, opposite Knockninny, and facing on the west the Cuilcagh, Bennaghlan and Florencecourt range of mountains, lies Corrard, the seat of Sir Charles Simeon King, Bart. (whose family is noticed under his property of Gola, also on the lake shore). It is surrounded on three sides by the lake. On the Down Survey map of the county, A.D. 1665, "Corrard," "Askall," and "Tomlohan" (subsequently Toneylaghan or Gubdarragh Point) appear as an island, and the headland "Inishbeg," *i.e.*, "Little Island," is another island. One of its three promontories bears the name of Friars' Point, and part of it is Friars' Field, which circumstance seems to indicate that it may have been one of the monastic retreats which once abounded on the shores and islands of Lough Erne. The old house was pulled down, *circa* 1825, preparatory to building a new one, but little more was done than to erect new offices, which were subsequently altered, and constitute the present residence.

[2] "Colcough" in MS. "Though generally considered as belonging to Leitrim and Cavan, it has its lofty eastern extremity, 2,188 feet high, altogether in Fermanagh. On the summit is a fine spring of excellent water. On this mountain, which is intimately associated with much of the legendary history of the district, the Maguires anciently invested their

These awful mountains, whose heads are generally wrapt in clouds, change the scene from beautiful to grand, and therefore afford a welcome diversification of the prospect to a person who, having sailed so far down the Lough, has had his eyes almost glutted with the repetition of so many and so charming landscapes.

This broad part of the Lough is interspersed with a multitude of islands, several of which are inhabited by husbandmen, others covered with cattle, most of them diversified with wood, ruins of old churches, houses, and the like.

The pleasantest of these islands is Belle Isle,[1] the

chiefs with supreme command over the adjacent country of Fermanagh."—Lewis's *Topog. Dict., Ireland*, 1837.

Upon the breast of Bennaghlan, in a singular position, is a monument erected by Lord Evelyn Stewart, to the memory of Mr. Maxwell.--Wakeman's (W. F.) *Lough Erne*, 1870.

[1] " A.D. 1498. MacManus of Seanadh, *i.e.*, Cathal Oge, the son of Cathal, son of Gillapatrick, son of Mathew, &c. A man who had kept a house of general hospitality, a *biatach*, at Seanadh-mic-manus, a canon chorister in Armagh, and in the Bishopric of Clogher, Parson of Inis-Cavin (Innishkeen), Deacon of Lough Erne, and coadjutor of the Bishop of Clogher, for fifteen years before his death, the repertory of the wisdom and science of his own country, fruitful branch of the Canón, and a fountain of charity and mercy to the poor and the indigent of the Lord : he it was who had collected together many historical books from which he had compiled the historical book, *Annales Senatenses*, or *Annals of Ulster of Baile-mic-manus*, for his own use, died of *galar breac* (smallpox), on the tenth of the calends of April, which fell on a Friday, and in the 60th year of his age." (*The Four Masters.*)—Archdall's *Monast. Hib.*, edited by Bishop Moran.

" Insul. vocat. McManus Island," &c., in Com. Fermanagh—Paul Gore, tenant—*Crown Rental*, 1623.

" Another (island) is Bally McManus, now called Bellisle, containing two large Tates, and much improved and Beautified at the Expenses of Sir Ralph Gore, Barrtt."—MS. *Hist. Fermanagh*, 1718-1719.

" Bellisle has long been celebrated for its natural beauties, which were much heightened by the judicious improvements

seat of the late Sir Ralph Gore[1]—one of the Lords
Justices of Ireland. It contains 200 plantation acres
of very good land, rising on every side from the water
in a gentle ascent. On the north side it is united to
the mainland by a large terrace, that was finished with
great labour—the Lough being, on each side of it, very
deep—there were planted along the sides of the terrace
rows of trees ; and a pallisade was carried along to pre-
vent passengers from falling into the water. On the

they received when it was the residence of the Earl of Ross : it
is connected with the main land by an elegant bridge.   Near it
is Lady Ross's Island, so called from the improvements be-
stowed on it by that lady.   Knockninny was used as a deer-
park by the nobleman just named."—Lewis's *Topog. Dict.*,
Ireland, 1837.

[1] " My horses foundered on Fermanagh ways ;
    Ways of well-polished and well-pointed stone,
    Where every step endangers every bone ;

    *   *   *   *   *   *   *   *   *   *

    But that the world would think I play'd the fool,
    I'd change with Charley Grattan for his school.
    What fine cascades, what vistoes might I make,
    Fix'd in the centre of the Iërnian lake !
    There might I sail delighted, smooth, and safe,
    Beneath the conduct of my good *Sir Ralph*,
    There's not a better steerer in the realm,
    I hope, my lord, you'll call him to the helm."

Dean Swift's " Epistle to H. E. Lord Carteret, 1729, by Rev.
Pat. Delany," ex-Fellow, T.C.D., and Rector of Derryvollan.

The Rt. Hon. Sir Ralph Gore, fourth Bart., of Manor Gore
(great-grandson of Sir Paul Gore, the first settler in Ireland,
created a Baronet of Ireland, in 1621), succeeded to his father's
Manor of Carrick, which includes Belleisle, on the death of his
mother, to whom it had been left for her life ; he mentions in
his will his farm at Knockninny, held by lease from Mr. Balfour ;
M.P. for Donegal Borough, 1703, 1709, and for Donegal Co., 1713,
1715, and for Clogher, 1727 ; P.C. ; Chancellor of the Exchequer ; elected Speaker, H. of Commons, 1729.   He *m.*,
1705, Elizabeth, daughter of Sir Richard Colvill, and by her

south side of the isle stands the house, which is but a
small lodge, chiefly agreeable for its situation ; from the
house descends, in an hanging level to the Lough, a
parterre, enclosed on the east and west sides with high
walls covered with fruit trees, and having on the ex-
tremities on each side square turrets, which hang over
the Lough : at the foot of the parterre is a quay, where
used to ride all kinds of pleasant boats.   Exactly frontward from the house, the islands—which are all wooded

---

(who died 1710) he had two daughters ; he *m.*, secondly,
Elizabeth (*d*. 1743), only daughter of St. George Ashe, D.D.,
Bishop, successively, of Clogher and Derry, and died 1733,
leaving issue.   His second son (who succeeded his eldest
brother, Sir St. George Gore St. George, fifth Bart., who *d. s. p.*
1746), Sir Ralph Gore, sixth Bart., a gallant soldier, who rose
to the rank of Lieut.-General, and Commander-in-chief in
Ireland, created, for his eminent services, Baron Gore, in 1746 ;
Viscount Belleisle, 1768 ; and Earl of Ross, 1771.   He had his
right arm shattered at Fontenoy, in 1745 ; he raised the
92nd Regiment of foot at his own expense ; *m.*, first, 1754,
Catherine, eldest sister of Right Hon. Thomas Conolly, she *d.*
s. p. v. 1771 ; he *m.*, secondly, his cousin Alice, daughter of
Right Hon. Nat. Clements (p. 2), and had by her a son,
Ralph, Viscount Belleisle, *b.* 1774 ; *d.* 1789.   Lord Ross, *d.*
circa 1802 (for further particulars relating to him and his family,
v. Lord Belmore's *Parliamentary Memoirs of Tyrone*, 1887),
and bequeathed his Manor of Carrick to his natural daughter,
Mary, who *m.*, 1798, Richard Hardinge, Esq., then Steward of
the Household to the Lord Lieutenant, and M.P. for Middleton,
created a Baronet, 1801.   Lady Hardinge *d. s. p.* in 1824.   The
Manor of Carrick was purchased by the late Rev. John Grey
Porter, Rector of Kilskeery, Co. Tyrone, eldest son of John
Porter, D.D., Bishop of Clogher (of an old Cumberland family) ;
and his son, the present proprietor, John Grey Vesey Porter,
Esq., of Belleisle, has much improved and beautified his seat,
and numerous islands, by judicious plantations.   To Mr. Porter's
enterprise the public are indebted for the well-appointed
steamers plying on the lake : and to his long-continued exertions
as sole promoter of a scheme for keeping the lake at a uniform
level, summer and winter, and so preventing disastrous floods,
it is due that this much-needed work has been so far carried
out.

and gently rising—are ranged so regularly on each hand,
that they, with the Lake between them, form the
appearance of a grand avenue planted in clumps.   This
avenue, on the water, is continued for three miles,
widening regularly as it removes from the house, and
terminates no less agreeably in the beautiful hill of
Knockninny.[1]

This hill alone is two miles in circumference ; it rises
in an oval form to the height of a mountain, and is
somewhat abrupt on the west side.   The soil of it is
reckoned not inferior to any of the county, being to the
very top clover ; it affords an extended prospect of all
the upper part of Lough Erne, from Belturbet to Enniskillen.   On the north side it is washed by the Lough ;
this side is enclosed in a deer-park, and has on the
shore stables and coach-houses, and a quay for boats ;
but its chief curiosity is a plentiful fountain of pure
water, which, being distilled through this large mountain
of gravel, has a clearness and coolness scarce to be met
with.   It is usual for company who have been pleasuring
on the Lough to retire to this fountain for their enter-
tainments, for which end around it are ranged benches
of sod,[2] and over it a shade of aquatic trees.   About ten
years ago, in digging on this hill, were found above a
score of brazen axes in a heap : they had on one end a
broad edge like the common hatchet, from which they
grew narrower, and tapered to a point : at the other
end there was no hole for the helve : the wood, instead
of embracing the axe, as is usual, was in these em-
braced by the axe ; they seem to be a kind of battle-

[1] See Appendix IV.

[2] "Sood" in MS.   A tourists' hotel now stands on the lake
shore by the quay.

axes, and were possibly made use of in war by persons who were not acquainted with the greater convenience of iron.

Maguire's River.

Two miles north-west from Lisnaskea Maguire's River enters Lough Erne. It rises in the County of Tyrone, not far from Clogher, thence running near Colebrooke, the seat of Henry Brooke, Esq.[1] It waters with its several branches that large vale of good soil that lies between the mountains Slieve Bagh[2] and the

---

[1] Governor of Fermanagh; Sheriff, 1709; M.P. for same county, 1727, till his death, 1761 [son of Major Thomas Brooke of Donegal (by Catherine, daughter of Sir John Cole, Bart., of Newlands, Co. Dublin, sister and co-heiress of Baron Ranelagh), who was son (by his second marriage, 1652, with Anne, daughter of Sir George St. George, Bart.) of Sir Henry Brooke, Knt., of Brookeborough; Captain of foot; M.P. for Donegal B., 1661; Sheriff, Fermanagh, 1669; who, for his services in 1641, was rewarded with a grant of land in Fermanagh; son of Sir Basil Brooke, Knt., of Borigall, the first settler in Ireland, one of the undertakers in the County Donegal, who *d*. 1633]. He *m*., 1711, Lettice (*d*. 1763), daughter of Alderman Benjamin Burton, of Dublin, and had issue—1. Sir Arthur, Sheriff for Fermanagh, 1752; M.P. for same county, 1761-1768, and 1776-1783; P.C., created, 1764, a Baronet of Ireland, but dying, 1785, *s. p. m.*, the dignity became extinct. 2. Francis, Major, Light Dragoons, *m.*, 1765, Hannah (*d*. 1819), daughter of Henry Prittie, Esq., of Kilboy, Co. Tipperary, and *d*. 1800, leaving six sons, of whom the eldest, Henry Brooke, of Colebrooke, Esq., created a Baronet in 1822, was father of Sir Arthur Brinsley Brooke, second Bart., and grandfather of the late Sir Victor Alexander Brooke, the third Bart., whose eldest son, Sir Arthur Douglas Brooke, is the present and fourth Bart.

[2] "Sliavh Beatha, surnamed from Bith, who was one of the 3 men y[t] accompanied Cessarea together wth 50 women to Ireland, 40 dayes before y[e] Deluge, and after they landed the women were divided in 3 squadrons betwixt these 3 men. Bith took his journey to y[e] north, and dyed on y[e] top of this mountaine, and was buried on y[e] carne on y[e] height thereof."—MS. *Hist. of Fermanagh*, 1718, 1719.

Topped[1] Mountain, thence passing through Maguire's Bridge,[2] it, a little lower, sinks into a deep, silent channel, and in this form twists and plays in an hundred meadows, through vast extended flats, for above three miles, till it enters Lough Erne, opposite to the north-east point of Knockninny. These flats are firm soil, clothed with a rich verdure, and covered with an infinite number of cattle. It is not easy to express the joy which this beautiful scene raises in one who rides a pleasuring along the banks of this river in the summer season. In the winter the scene is entirely changed. Lough Erne spreads over all up to the town of Lisnaskea and near to Maguire's Bridge. These vast verdant flats become so many spacious bays, and the little hills that here and there are scattered through them are made islands.

Almost opposite to the mouth of this river, about two miles northward from Knockninny, on the western side of the lake, is the mouth of the Duanim, or River of Stragownah.

River Duanim, or Stragownah.

It rises from a large lake near Bawnboy, the seat of John Enery, Esq.,[3] in the north-west part of the County of Cavan; issuing thence it is swelled with a great number of brooks tumbling down from the mountains of Cuilcagh on the west, and those of Slieve Russell on the south-east. In the course of five

---

[1] Topped Mt., anciently Mullagh Knock—"the hill on the hill"—909 feet above the level of the sea, with a cairn on the top of it.

[2] Near this town is Drumgoon, the seat of Francis J. Graham, Esq., D.L.

[3] See p. 25, note, for some account of this family. " Patrick Enery, of Swanlinbar," was living in 1690.

miles it sweeps by the small market-town of Swanlinbar,[1] where once was a great iron-work ; hence it flows in a course of three miles to the Bridge of Stragownah, which is a mile southward from Kinawly, and thence in two miles more it opens into Lough Erne. The whole course of this river is about ten miles, the last five through a deep morass. As it is supplied by mountain brooks, it swells in floods to a great height. It affords great plenty of large trouts. Some time ago there were forests of oak along the banks of this river ; but they have been so entirely extirpated in order to supply the iron-works at Swanlinbar, that there is scarce a stump left. In all the bogs and morasses round it are found great, huge trunks of oak.

RIVER ARNEY.

Two miles northward from the mouth of the Duanim flows into the lake the large and pleasant River Arney. It rises out of Lurganna Colley[2] mountains, in the

[1] " Swadlinbar " in MS. " There is likewise a famous town where the worst iron in the kingdom is made, and it is called *Swandlingbar*, the original of which name I shall explain, lest the antiquaries of future ages might be at a loss to derive it. It was a most witty conceit of four gentlemen who ruined themselves with this iron project : *Sw* stands for *Swift*, *And* for *Sanders*, *Ling* for *Darling*, and *Bar* for *Barry*. Methinks I see the four loggerheads sitting in consult, like *Smectymnuus*, each gravely contributing a part of his own name to make up one for their place in the ironwork, and could wish they had been hanged as well as undone for their wit."—Dean Swift, *On Barbarous Denominations in Ireland*, 1728.

The ore came from the neighbouring mountain, Cuilcagh, and the works were continued till the supply of timber failed. The town possesses a mineral spring strongly impregnated with sulphur, &c. Its waters were in high esteem as a restorative from debility, and the spa was at one time much resorted to.

Sir John Dunbar and Sir Leonard Blennerhassett erected iron-works on their estates in Fermanagh.

[2] Or " Lugnacuillagh," 1,485 feet high.

County of Leitrim, about three miles eastward from the
town of Manor Hamilton ; thence tumbling down
through Glin Farm, it enters into a great lake called

LOUGH MACNANE, OR MACNEAN,

from the multitudes of fowl that frequent it ; this
lake is about nine miles in length from west to east, and
in its western and broadest end, three miles broad, filling
up the whole bottom that lies between the mountains
of Dubally on the south, the Doows and Slieve-MacGla-
naghy on the west, and Belmore[1] on the north.   It is
divided into two parts ; the western part, spreading
wide, contains several large islands, some of which have
great woods.   In one of them is a yew wood.   Near the
southern shore stands the ruins of a large old castle in
the water, built on a single rock that stands near half a
mile out in the lough ; it was the seat of the Macga-
verins, the ancient proprietors of the country.   Two
miles more easterly stands on the same side the old
parish church of Killinah, near to which runs a large
rivulet, which sometimes merges under ground, again
rises and continues the frolicsome course of hiding and
seeking till it enters the lake.   The whole country
around this upper part of Lough Macnane is exceeding
wild and mountainous—the interspersion of islands and
points of good land shooting into the lake makes the
whole scene pleasant and romantic.   This lake, having
continued broad for five miles, is contracted into a

[1] 1,312 feet high.   The Scottish-descended family of Lowry-
Corry, of Castle Coole, near Enniskillen, take the title of their
Earldom and Barony from this mountain.   The fourth and
present Earl of Belmore, K.C.M.G., &c., is author of the *Hist.
of the Manors of Finagh and Coole*, 1881 ; and *Parliamentary
Memoirs of Fermanagh and Tyrone*, 1887.

narrow, deep canal, in which form it flows through a flat
meadow for half a mile to the redoubt of Bellcoe, where
is a good ford and a new bridge across it. From the
ford the lake, expanding again, continues for three
miles more in length, and a good mile in breadth. The
country about this lower lake, growing pleasanter,
beautifies the lake with several points of good land
shooting out far into it. In the very midst of the
broadest part of this lake stands a small circular island,
overgrown with shrubs and bushes ; it is about two
hundred paces in circumference, and formed into a very
strong, Danish fortification, having a high dike and
foss encompassing the whole : it is now the habitation
of herons, but it was, in ancient times, a stronghold,
and might, if there was any occasion, be made impreg-
nable for a trifling expense, it being on all sides out of
the reach of shot from the mainland. But the principal
ornament and grandeur of this lake (Macnane) is
derived from the prodigious Rock of Gortatowell, whose
abrupt brow, rising to the height of 600 feet at least,
hangs as a huge cliff over the south-east end of the
lake. The top of this stupendous rock has a steep
walk ; its front is diversified with yew and ivy, and its
scalp bare ; its eastern end is adorned with a small ash
wood, that creeps up the steep ; out of its western end
issues the subterraneous rivulet of Gortawell Mill,
before mentioned, and just under the brow of the cliff,
between it and the lake, lies the great new road leading
towards Sligo. It is usual for passengers to stop here
and admire the awful majesty of the cliff hanging over
them, and the huge lumps of rock that have tumbled
down from it, and to entertain themselves with the
extraordinary echo frequently reverberated between the

lake below and the hollowness of the cliff. About this cliff, as also those of Dubally, farther westward on the lake, are yet eagles of the largest kind, choice hawks, and Cornish daws, with red shanks and red bills, which are much sought after by the curious. This rock is reckoned one of the bars of Killesher: it and the adjacent hills are so covered with all kinds of wholesome herbs that the whey of the vast herds of goats which browse along them is reckoned equal to that on the mountains of Mourne. A quarter of a mile from the cliff, on the east end, stands the parish church of Killesher, and a little below it Lough Macnane terminates.

River Arney.

From the east end of the lake the River Arney again issues out and continues its course through a corkous marsh, for a mile, till it receives, at right angles on the south side, the rapid river which tumbles down from the Marble Arch before mentioned, and is called the Claddagh River. From thence it holds its course eastward for six miles, through bogs and deep marshes, till it opens beautifully into Lough Erne, at Clonurson, a farm on the glebe of Killesher. The depth of this river (Arney) affords a free navigation, especially in the winter, between these two great loughs, Macnane and Erne, and might contribute greatly to the improvement of the country, if there was any trade to encourage it. It abounds much with large, high-tasted trouts, and is one of the principal rivers of Lough Erne for the salmon retiring to spawn. Several tons of these spent salmon used to be taken in October and November, by spreading nets across the mouth of the river at Clonurson,

and killing them in other places of the shallows ; but
the incumbent of Killesher thought it his duty to put a
stop to a wicked practice, so detrimental to the public,
and no less a robbery of the gentlemen to whom the
fishery of Lough Erne belongs.

LOUGH ERNE.

Opposite to the mouth of Arney River lies Innismore[1]
or the Great Island—so called because it is the greatest

[1] "He (Bishop Spottiswood) recovered also other lands his
predecessor, Bishop (George) Montgomerie, was never in pos-
session of, as, namely, the Isle of Devenishe, from the Lord
Hastings, and the greatest part of the Island Inishmore, from
Sir Ralph Goore, Baronett."—*Life of James Spotswood, Lord
Bishop of Clochar. Hay's Memoirs,* 1700 (MS., Advocates'
Library).

"In one of the greatest Islands of Lough Earn (Innismore ?),
Sir Henry Spotteswood (son of the Bishop) had a fine seat with
goodly buildings, gardens, orchards, and a pretty little village,
with a church and steeple belonging to it, which, whether it is
in being yet, or destroyed by the barbarians and bloody rebels,
I am not informed."—*Natural Hist. of Ireland,* by Gerard
Boate, 1652.

Innismore is connected on its east side, near Gola, with the
mainland, by Carry Bridge, and a viaduct is now (1892) in progress to unite it on the west side at Clontycoora.

The following lines are from the pen of the Rev. J. W. Kaye,
LL.D., Rector of Derrybrusk, to whom the public are indebted
for several charming poetic illustrations of the beauties of
Lough Erne scenery :—

"CARRY BRIDGE."

A Reverie.

" One summer eve I wander'd on
    By lough, and mead, and ferry,
Until I came and stood alone
    Upon the bridge of Carry.
I gazed below upon the flow
    Of waters rolling under :
My thoughts ran fast upon the past,
    And fill'd my mind with wonder.

in all Lough Erne; being of a circular form, and about five miles in circuit; it has on the southern side a large land lough—in form of a great basin—which has a communication with the great Lough by a deep, narrow gut. This island is an excellent soil and well inhabited : the sailing round it is very pleasant. Opposite

" I thought of deeds in years gone by,
    When brothers fought with brothers ;
  When kings waged war with chieftain lords—
    O'Neils, Maguires, and others ;
  And if they fought near here, I thought,
    'Midst all their flight and flurry,
  Where would they go ?—for then you know
    There was no bridge at Carry.

" I thought of good St. Patrick too,
    Who oft, in Innismore,
  Would preach to crowds assembled round
    From hill, and dale, and shore ;
  And there's the stone, ' worn to the bone,'
    Where oft all night he'd tarry
  In earnest prayer, in Arda there,
    Whene'er he pass'd through Carry.

" I look'd across to Gola then,
    Where once the Abbey stood ;
  I thought of monks who counted beads
    In prayerful, solemn mood ;
  I could not name how oft they came
    With net and " cot " or wherry,
  As Fridays pass'd and Lenten fast,
    To catch their fish at Carry.

*   *   *   *   *   *   *

" But twilight falls, and seems to hide
    The visions of the past ;
  The ancient feudal times are gone—
    'Tis well they could not last ;
  And chiefs ne'er wield the sword and shield,
    Nor desperate spear-thrusts parry :
  'Tis well 'tis so. Flow, waters, flow
    Beneath the bridge of Carry."

to its north-east corner stands Gola,[1] the seat of Charles
King,[2] Esq.

[1] " Golan " in MS.—" Gola," the " river forks." " Gaulæ
adhuc videre est aliqua antiqui Cænobii Rudera. Modernus
Fundi Dominus est Jacobus King, Armiger."—*Hibernia Domi-
nica*, by Dr. Thos. Burke, 1762.
" Adjoining Lough Erne, a monastery for Dominican Friars
was founded and dedicated to (the Nativity of) the Blessed
Virgin, by MacManus, lord of the place, of which there are
still some remains, also traces of the village of Gola in which it
was situated."—Lewis's *Topog. Dict., Ireland*, 1837.
Any remains of the *ancient* monastery are most probably now
to be found in the farm-house belonging to the daughters of the
late Mr. Robert Wilson, who died 1890 (the purchaser from the
landlord, Sir Charles S. King, Bart., of his farms, under Lord
Ashbourne's Act), which is part of the house occupied as a
residence by the elder branch of the King family for a hundred
years.
The date of this Abbey's foundation is not recorded. Aldfred,
King of the Northumbrian Saxons, is stated to have learned
here to speak and write in the Gaelic tongue ; and his poem in
praise of Erin is still extant. It is not returned in the great
survey of Fermanagh, made at Devenish, 7 July, 1603 ; and in
the Inquisition at Inniskillen, 18 Sept., 1609, to enquire into
ecclesiastical lands, the only mention of the place is that it was
then part of the *herinagh* lands of Derrybrusk. On the 1609
map of " Barony of Magherysteffanah," it appears as an
ecclesiastical edifice on the townland " eclamre," next " tate-
goule " (Gola), and " farranouollan " (Farnamullan). In the
Down Survey Map, 1665, the townland is recorded as " Givola."
Dr. Burke describes the convents as suppressed in 1649, and
restored at the Restoration. Subsequently to the latter event,
Fathers Cathal MacManus and Thos. MacMahon erected a *new
house* at Gola, near the ancient abbey, under the patronage of
MacManus, probably a descendant of the original founder. This
accounts for the existence of a monastery here so late as the
18th century, while the old Abbey was the residence of the
King family. In 1756 John Maguire, aged 55, was Prior, and
Thos. Nolan, aged 60, and Antony Maguire, aged 50, Brethren.
(Partly from Archdall's *Monasticum Hib.*, edited, with notes by
P. Moran, D.D., 1873.)
" Mr. John King remains in yᵉ handsome seate of Gola in
this Co."—MS. *Hist. of Fermanagh*, 1718, 1719.

[2] The author is in error in describing Gola as seat of "Charles"
King : it was that of his elder brother, James, who had settled

Below Innismore the Lough resumes the form of a
spacious, silent river, and in this form embraces in its
arms Cleenish Isle.   This island is about three miles

Corrard (p. 42) on his brother Charles, on the latter's marriage
in 1731.

James King [a representative of the ancient house of Barra,
in the Garioch, Aberdeenshire, of which a cadet, Sir James
King, of Birness, Lieut.-General to Gustavus Adolphus and
King Charles I., was, by the latter, raised to the peerage of
Scotland, in 1642, as Lord Eythin (extinct)] settled in Fer-
managh, *temp*. Car. I.   His name does not appear in the Crown
Rental for 1643, and there is none for Ulster between that
date and 1653, in which year his name appears for lands in
the Baronies of Magherastephinagh, Tyrkennedy, and Lurg.
He acquired freehold property in Enniskillen from Michael
Cole, Esq., and is described as " of Corrard," in a deed dated
15th August, 1674 ; he probably died soon after that date.
He *m*. Nicholas Johnston, and had issue eight sons and two
daughters—I. James King, Esq., of Corrard and Dublin, took
refuge in England in 1689 ; *d. s. p*. Mar. 2, 1726, leaving his
Fermanagh estates to the three sons of his brother John, and his
Meath property to his nephew, James (subsequently Sir James)
Somerville.   II. Robert King, of Lissen Hall, near Swords,
agent to his cousin, William King, Archbishop of Dublin (Appendix II.), whom he visited during the latter's imprisonment,
in 1689.   He appears to have escaped from Dublin to the Duke
of Schomberg's camp, near Lisburn, " to whom he gave an
account of how things stood at Dublin," 22nd Jan., 1689-90 ;
M.P. for Lifford, 1698-1703, and 1709, till his death in 1711 ;
m. Marion Hamill, of the house of Roughwood, Ayrshire, and
had issue two daughters : 1. Anne, *m*., 1700, first wife, Robert
Ross, Esq., *jure uxoris* of Rosetrevor, Co. Down, M.P., and
had issue ; 2. Mary (*d*. 1733), ward to Archbishop King, *m*.,
1713, William Smyth, Esq., of Drumcree, Westmeath, *jure
uxoris* of Monea Manor, Co. Fermanagh, Sheriff for latter Co.,
1736, M.P., and had issue.   III. John King, of whom subsequently.   IV. William King.   V. Charles King, attainted in
his absence from Ireland, 1689, *m*. Katherine, sister of Robert
Galbraith, of Cloncorick, Co. Leitrim (heir of James Galbraith,
of Balgair), and *d*. 1714, leaving issue two sons ; 1. Robert, of
Drewstown, Co. Meath, and Raven Hill, Co. Armagh, Esq.,
m. his cousin, Anne (*d*. 1739), daughter of Rev. Thomas King,
of Swords (and widow of Captain Robert Hassard, of Mount
Hassard, Co. Fermanagh, Sheriff for his Co., 1719), and *d*.
1760, leaving two daughters, co-heiresses : Catherine, the
eldest, *m*., 1761, his first wife, Sir James Nugent, first Bart. of

in circuit—some part of it tilled, but the far greater
part grazed with black cattle, for which the extended
flats that are around its shores render it very convenient.

Donore, and *d. s. p.* 1787; Margaret, the second daughter, *m.*
Barry, Earl of Farnham (p. 5); 2. John, of Mossfield, Co.
Tyrone, Esq. (for whose issue *vide* Lord Belmore's *Parliamentary Memoirs of Co. Tyrone, s. v.* "John King, Esq., M.P.,
Clogher, 1800"). VI. Rev. Thomas King, M.A., Prebendary
of Swords; born in Fermanagh, 1663; imprisoned by King
James's Government in Newgate, Dublin, 1689; *m.* Elizabeth
(*d.* 1731), daughter and heiress of John Bernard, Esq., of
Drumin, Co. Louth (and widow of Rev. John Archdale, Vicar
of Lusk, 1679-1690), and *d.* 1709, leaving issue. VII. Crom-
well King. VIII. David King, Esq., Sheriff of Dublin, 1716-17;
at his house in Skinner's Row a large quantity of the Public
Records were secreted during the Revolution; *m.,* 1696-7,
Anne Weir (*d.* 1755, *æt.* 78), and *d.* 1737, leaving issue (extinct).
The two daughters (of James King, the first of Corrard) were: I.
Katherine King, *m.* Thomas Somerville, Alderman of Dublin,
third son of Thomas Somerville (*d.* 1669), of Drumadown, Co.
Fermanagh [and Jean, his spouse, daughter of James Warnock,
of Enniskillen; she *m.* secondly Robert Galbraith, attainted
1689, and had issue by him], third son of James Somerville, of
Tullykelter, Co. Fermanagh (*d.* 1642), of the house of Cambus-
nethan, Ayrshire (and his wife, Elizabeth, daughter of Thomas
Hamilton, of Brimhill); she *d.* 1725, leaving issue by her husband, Alderman Somerville (who *d.* 1718), one son, Sir James
Somerville, Knt., ancestor of the Barons Athlumney and
Meredyth, and four daughters. II. Elizabeth King, *m.* Captain
Robert Clarke, of Inniskilling, who was one of the five who
first took arms to defend that town against King James's troops,
and raised a company for the purpose; he was attainted 1689;
she left issue by her husband, who *d.* 1716.

The aforenamed John King, of Gola, Esq., probably took
part in the defence of Enniskillen in 1689, as his name appears
in the list of signatories to the address to King William
and Queen Mary from that town in 1690 (Appendix II.); he
m. —— —— (*vivens* 1711), and *d.* 1720-26, leaving issue three
sons: I. James King, of Gola, Esq., Sheriff for the county,
1728, who presented the communion plate to Derryvollan
Church (p. 58); Clerk (1749) of the Forfeitures, Dublin; *m.,*
first, Margaret Irwin, or Irvine, who *d.,* 1735, *s. p.;* secondly,
Katherine, daughter of William Gore, D.D., Dean of Down,
uncle of the Earl of Ross (p. 45), and *d.* 1756, leaving issue
two sons and one daughter, viz.: 1. James, of Gola, Captain,
1760, in the 92nd (Lord Ross's) Regiment, and, in 1761, in

In it are the ruins of the parish church, which takes its name from the island.

Adjoining to this is another large island, Inniskeen;[1] in this, also, are the ruins of an old church.

At the north end of a long, broad canal, which shoots down from Innismore, between Cleenish to the west, and Derrybrusk[2] to the east, stands on a hill the Church of Derryvullan,[3] and adjoining to it the seat of John

20th Foot, retired 1772 ; *m*. his cousin (ward to Lord Ross), Elizabeth, only daughter of Chidley Coote, of Mount Coote, Co. Limerick, Esq., and *d*., leaving an only son, James, in H. E. I. Co.'s service, Secretary to Board of Trade, Bengal, who *d. s. p. l.* in London, 1823-6 ; Gola was purchased, 1815, by his cousin, Abraham Bradley King, Esq. ; 2. William, Major, 58th, *d. s. p.; 1.* Hannah Honora, *m.,* 1764, Edward Sneyd, Esq., M.P., and had issue (p. 24). II. Charles King, of Corrard, Fermanagh, Esq., *m.,* 1731, Elizabeth (*d.* 1790), daughter of Rev. James Cottingham, M.A., of Ardmagh, Co. Cavan (by Mary, daughter of Rev. William Greene, of Dresternan, Fermanagh (p. 15), and *d.* 1788. His grandson, the aforenamed Abraham Bradley King, Esq., of Corrard, created a Baronet in 1821, was father of the Rev. Sir James Walker King, second Baronet, and grandfather of Sir Charles Simeon King, third and present Bart. III. Robert King, of Derrybrusk, Co. Fermanagh, *vivens* 1736, *d. s. p.,* leaving a widow.

[1] " Enniskean " in MS. " Inis-Caoin," the beautiful island. The town of Enniskillen was formerly included in this parish. Canon Bradshaw records, in *Enniskillen Long Ago*, that vestry meetings were held in this old church down to the year 1738.

[2] Derrybrusk House, successively belonging to the Montgomerys and to the Deerings, was purchased by the late R. Hall, Esq., J.P., and re-named Innismore Hall ; it is now the seat of his representatives, George Gray, Esq., and Mrs. Gray.

[3] A handsome service of communion plate (tankard, chalice, and paten), engraved with his family arms, crest, and motto, was presented to this church by James King, Esq., of Gola (p. 57), which was formerly in this parish, and bears the inscription " Ex dono Jacobi King de Gola, arm⁸, Ecclesiæ de Derrwoylan, A.D. 1727." Since the division of the old parish into two new ones, in 1874, the mother church, where this plate is still in use, is named Derryvollan South.

Rynd,[1] Esq., which is well shaded with trees, and commands a prospect of this spacious canal and the adjoining islands.

Below Derryvullan, the several small arms of the Lough which circulate round these islands are gathered into one serpentine canal, which makes a beautiful meander o, near a mile round Rind MacMorrish, that is, FitzMaurice Point, that shoots out from the east side of the Lough almost in the form of an horse-shoe. On the west side shoots out another point which indents with this.

Below these points, the Lake, continuing in the form of a spacious serpentine river, bends under the old Abbey and Castle of Lisgoole.[2] The situation of this

[1] This surname is Scottish, and frequently to be met with on the Perth Registers. The first of the family in this county appears to have been "David Rynd, of Inniskillinge, the elder." He was a commonwealth tenant of the lands of Carrow in 1659 ; m. Margaret (d. 1675, æt. 67, buried at Enniskillen, where is a tablet to her memory), daughter of Christopher Irvine, Esq., widow of Colonel Richard Bell, and of Captain Thomas Maxwell (Canon Bradshaw's *Enniskillen Long Ago*, 1878). He was buried at Enniskillen, 1677, leaving issue— David Rynd, Esq., of Derryvollan, Sheriff for his county, 1681 ; Provost, Enniskillen, 1682; attainted, 1689 ; d. 1723, leaving issue by Margaret, his wife, three daughters and three sons, of whom the younger were Christopher, and Thomas, of Dublin, merchant (will proved, 1709) ; and the eldest, John Rynd, Esq., of Derryvollan, and Dartry, Co. Leitrim, Sheriff for Fermanagh, 1708, d. 1746, æt. 73, leaving issue one daughter and five sons, the younger were Rev. James Rynd, of Derryvollan (will proved 1746), Thomas, John, Richardson ; and the eldest, David Rynd, Esq., of Derryvollan ; Sheriff, 1745 ; m., 1746, Mary, daughter of Oliver Moore, Esq., of Sanlistown, and d. (will proved 1758), leaving issue an only child, Mary (d. 1774), m., 1769, Edward Denny, Esq., M.P., Tralee (d. 1775), brother of Sir Barry Denny, first Bart., of Tralee Castle, and by her was ancestor of Rev. Edward Denny, M.A., the present Vicar of Kempley, Dymock, Glos.

[2] "Lisgold" in MS. In the early ages of Christianity a monastery was founded at Lisgoole ; and afterwards, in 1106,

seat is equally august and charming, for it stands on
the top of a beautiful evergreen hill that rises steep, but
not abrupt, over the Lake on its west side, and from
this eminence commands a large prospect of this
serpentine canal in its several circlings and indentures.
The Castle was once a place of strength, but was
destroyed in the rebellion of 1641 by the Macguires,
who stained it with the blood of above one hundred
Protestants—men, women, and children—whom they
killed and burned to death in it at once; since that
time it has lain in ruins.[1]

From Lisgoole the Lake—which hitherto flowed
northward—changes its course a little, and bends westward for the remaining part of its course.

an abbey for Augustinians, by O'Neil, King of Ulster, on its
site. In 1360 this abbey was burnt down. Early in the 16th
century, Fitzcuchonnaght Maguire, Lord of Fermanagh, agreed
to rebuild it ; but before its completion, in 1530, Henry VIII.
dissolved monastic institutions (Canon Bradshaw's *Enniskillen
Long Ago*). Mr. Wakeman, in *Lough Erne*, 1870, gives the
inscription on a chalice presented "by Sir Bryan Maguire,
Knight of the Noble Order Militaire of St. Louis, for y⁰ use of
yᵉ convent of Lisgoole, in the Co. of Fermanagh, near Enniskillen, A.D. 1739." This proves that the Abbey of Lisgoole,
like that of Gola, continued in existence to a comparatively
recent period.

Sir John Davis, Knt., had an assignment of Lisgoole from
Sir Henry Bruncker, the patentee, in 1606, and, on his death,
in 1630, it passed to his daughter, Lucy, and her husband,
Ferdinando, Lord Hastings.

John Armstrong, Esq., of Lisgoole, *m.*, 1788, Sophia,
daughter of 9th Baron Blayney, and had issue an only child,
Elizabeth, *m.*, 1808, Sir Charles Dodsworth, 3rd Bart. of New-
land Park, Co. York; she *d.* 1853, and was grandmother of the
present Sir Charles E. Dodsworth, 5th Bart. "The Armstrong-
Blayney marriage gave Miss R. M. Roche the idea of her story
of 'The Children of the Abbey.'"—(Lt.-Gen. G. S. Montgomery's *Hist. of Montgomery of Ballyleck*, &c.).

Lisgoole was the residence of Mrs. Jones, who died this year
(1892). Some portion of the old Abbey is incorporated in the
present house.

[1] Opposite Lisgoole is Bellevue, the handsome seat of Capt.
Wm. Collum, D.L.

Below Lisgoole the Lough flows for a mile in the form of a river to Scarlet's Weir. Here it is so contracted between two gravelly banks that it is not above a hundred paces over; it quickens also into a small stream, and is so shallow in a dry summer that large boats pass with difficulty. At this weir are taken in the summer season great quantities of salmon,[1] and in the beginning of winter great quantities of large silver eels, but the damage done to the public by it, and the shallow ford on which it stands, is exceeding great, for it is in this strait and ford which dams up all the upper part of Lough Erne, and causes it to overflow so many rich lands. I may venture to say, that it would be very practicable for a small expense laid out in removing this weir and cutting the ford deeper, so to sink the upper part of the Lake as to recover several thousand acres of the richest land in the country which are overflowed a great part of the year, and so to reform the many marshes as to make them become in a short time choice land.[2]

[1] " Formerly the people and gentry of the country had salmon at a very easy rate at sixpence per piece ; . . . . but since the Revolution they either can't have them at all, or at what they count an excessive rate."—*Of the Salmon Fishing of Ireland*, by His Grace (Wm. King, D.D.) the Abp. of Dublin, in Boate's *Natural Hist. of Ireland*, 1726.

[2] " The navigation of the Shannon, if it were once vigorously and effectually carried on, and the cutting a canal from Lough Erne to the seaport of Ballyshannon, would be two undertakings of vast advantage to our inland commerce, and indeed the last would be so feasible, and have such effects on that part of the kingdom, that it cannot long be overlooked."—*Reflections and Resolutions Proper for the Gentlemen of Ireland, &c.*, by Rev. Sam. Madden, D.D., 1738.

The plan for keeping the Lough at a nearly uniform level, summer and winter, promoted by Mr. J. G. V. Porter, of Belleisle (p. 45), and carried out by the Local Drainage Board from 1880 to 1891, has been not that here proposed by Dr. Madden,

The Lough, being disentangled from this difficult strait, receives on its south side Sillies River[1]—before mentioned—which twists into it through a broad corkous meadow, and expands itself again into an easy spreading bay under the Church of Rossory, half a mile below which it circles round the so much celebrated town and island of Enniskillen.[2]

This town is the metropolis and only borough in the county of Fermanagh. It is most charmingly situated, being built on a small oblong island, which consists of two little hills and a few flat skirts, which are overflowed in winter. The whole island is scarcely half a mile in length, and a quarter in breadth. At each end it is joined to the mainland by a large stone bridge. That branch of Lough Erne which flows by its western end is the deepest and largest, and is the general

but one more in accord with the author's suggestion, viz. : the removal of obstructions such as shoals and stones, the cutting and dredging of deep channels where needful, the removal of the old eel weir at Belleek, and the cutting of the falls there, and the erection of four sluices on the site of the crest of the falls, these sluices being each 29 feet 4 inches wide, 14 feet deep, and capable of being raised 9 feet high from an overhead bridge. Owing to the excessive cost entailed in the execution of the works, amounting with interest on the money spent, to £181,557 16s. 0d., in addition to a Treasury grant of £30,000 for navigation purposes, the material benefit to those interested will be neutralized by the heavy assessments payable for 49 years from 10 Oct., 1890.

[1] " Syllys " in MS. It rises in the mountains near Church Hill, parish of Innismacsaint, and is a considerable river, partly navigable.

[2] "The name as spelt in Irish is Inis Caithlen, or Caithlinn, *i.e.*, the Isle of Kehlen. In the ' Annals of Clonmacnoise ' it is stated that this island took its name from Cethlen (Kehlen), wife of Balor of the great blows, chief of the Fomorians, a race of pirates who infested the coasts of Ireland, and oppressed the inhabitants far into the interior."—Canon Bradshaw's *Enniskillen Long Ago*, 1878.

passage of great boats, for which end the piers of the
bridge are raised high, and the arches are left wide.
The bridge[1] on the western branch has a square tower,
with a gateway and guard-room standing in the midst;
the other, on the eastern,[2] had once a draw-bridge.

The figure which this town makes to the eye bears
no proportion to the great figure it has made in history.
It consists of one broad street, which reaches along the
ridge of the hills from bridge to bridge, and of a few
alleys and gardens that descend to the Lake on
both sides. There are scarcely in the whole town
150 houses, and most of these but indifferent cabins, it
not having yet recovered from the flames which reduced
it to ashes about thirty years ago (Appendix II.). Its
principal buildings are the Castle, the seat of the Coles,[3]

[1] A new bridge, "The Erne Bridge," has been recently
erected here by the Lough Erne Drainage Board.

[2] The draw-bridge was put up in 1688.

[3] The representative in 1739 of this ancient Devonshire
family, and great-great-grandson of Sir William Cole, Knt., the
first settler in Ireland, and founder of the modern town of Enniskillen, who died in 1653, was John Cole, Esq., Sheriff of Fermanagh, 1733; M.P., Enniskillen, 1729, till he was created in 1760
Baron Mountflorence, of Florencecourt (p. 14) in the Peerage of
Ireland; m., 1728, Elizabeth, daughter of Hugh Willoughby
Montgomery, Esq., of Carrow, Co. Monaghan, and d. 1767, leaving,
with two daughters, two sons, of whom the eldest, William
Willoughby, succeeded as second Baron, and was created, 1776,
Viscount Enniskillen, and, in 1789, Earl of Enniskillen; his
son, John Willoughby, second Earl, had the Barony of Grin-
stead in the peerage of the U. K. conferred upon him, 1815.
The third and late Earl (son of the second Earl), William
Willoughby, was a great lover of geological science; a Fellow
of the Geological Society of London, 1828, and one of the oldest
members of the Geological Club; a Fellow of the Royal Society,
1829; and a member of the Royal Irish Academy; a D.C.L.,
and LL.D., of Trinity College, Dublin. The collection of fossil
fishes formed by his lordship was one of the most complete
probably in the world. He published, in 1869, an *Alphabetical*

who are proprietors of the town, and a great part of the country around. It stands beautifully over the Lake, at the western end of the town, a little above the bridge. It was once strong and capacious, but is now in ruins. A little above this, on the top of the western hill, stands the Church,[1] which is a large and strong old building. From its steeple there is a delightful prospect of the Lough and the country around. Under the Church, on the northern side of the town, by the

Catalogue of the Type Specimens of Fossil Fishes in the Collection of the Earl of Enniskillen. When Lord Cole, he appears to have worked zealously with Sir Philip de Malpas Grey Egerton, Bart., associated with whom he published *A Systematic and Stratigraphical Catalogue of Fossil Fish* in both their collections. He *d.* 1886, *æt.* 80, and was succeeded by his eldest surviving son, Lowry Egerton, the present and fourth Earl of Enniskillen.

[1] Of the church erected in 1637 the tower alone remains. The present edifice was completed in 1842. The Rector at the time of the old church's erection was John Smith, who subsequently retired to England, and died at Bondgate, Co. York, in 1652, and a tablet was placed to his memory in Ripon Cathedral. In his will, dated 8th Feb., 1652, is the following quaint "memo." :—"That my wife (Deborah) hath in her custody a chalice and cover for it, wch Mr. Edward Davis, at my request, gave to the use of the Church of Inisskillin, and is to bee restored to that Church when the parrishioners shall pay my Executrix fouer pounds, six shillings, eight pence, which I layd out for them in paveinge and plasteringe the said churche." This chalice, still in use in Enniskillen Church, bears the inscription—" Poculum Ecclesiæ Parochialis de Eniskeene, ex dono Edvardi Davis generosi, anno 1638." It is noteworthy that John Smith mentions as his brothers-in-law "Dr. Margettson " (Query ? the subsequent Archbishop of Dublin, and, on the death of John Bramhall, Primate of Ireland), and " Mr. William Bramhall ;" and " John Bramhall " is a witness. The two future Primates were natives of Yorkshire, and had both taken refuge in England. A Sunday School was instituted " at Enniskillen under the patronage of Sir James Caldwell, Bart., and Jas. Hall, Esq., (which now consists of 180 children), who pay James Kiernan £18 4s. for superintending the school." (*Dublin Chronicle*, Aug. 7, 1788).

Lough, stands the School.[1] It is the best endowed
with lands of any school in Ireland. On the top of
the eastern hill, which is the principal part of the town,
is a square where the markets are held. On one side
of this square stands a Barrack for two companies of
foot. At the eastern end of the town, near the bridge,
stands a large Court-house, under which is a strong
vaulted gaol. Nor is this town much more remarkable
for strength than buildings. It has neither walls nor
dike nor any other advantage, but what it derives from
its being an island; nor is this very great, as the Lake on
each end is but narrow, and the hills on the mainland
command it. Two of these hills—one hanging over each
end of the town—seem to be of great importance to
preserve: that on the west side rises high from the end
of the bridge; it has on each side a large land lough,

[1] Founded in 1627, it was removed, 1777, to Portora.

" Enniskillen, 22nd Jan., 1629. Richard Boorke, Master of
the Free Schoole of the Co. Fermanagh, by himselfe and his
ushers, hath diligently executed and discharged the place or
office of a schoole-master at Ballibalfore in the said Co. for
2 yeares until the 15th June last 1629, or thereabouts, since
which tyme, for the most parte, he hath discontinued the
keeping thereof in his owne pson, but, since that time, hath
left two Ushers to instruct the schollers. The number of
schollers in the said schoole now are three score or thereabouts,
all except 3 beinge Irish natives."—*Inquisitions, Co. Fermanagh.*

Mr. Thomas Dunbar, a subsequent master, *m.* Catherine,
4th daughter of Alexander Conyngham, Dean of Raphoe
(widow of James Leslie (p. 23), attainted 1689, and *d. s. p.*
1690-5.

" The Free School now (1719) under the care and tuition of
Mr. Charles Grattan."—MS. *Hist. of Fermanagh.* Mr. Grattan,
M.A., ex-F.T.C.D. (p. 44), died 1746, and was succeeded by Rev.
William Dunkin, D.D., who had been Latin Master of St.
Michael's le Pole, Dublin—" the best English, as well as Latin,
poet in this kingdom."— SWIFT.

between which and Lough Erne there are narrow passes, so that by this situation this hill commands the two only approaches to the town on that side : the other at the eastern end is stronger and of more consequence ; it rises from the end of the bridge regularly in the form of a cone ; it is steep and has on its south side the Lough, and around the rest of its bottom a corkous marsh ; on the top is built a strong fort of sods, which commands all around ; from this there is cut a covered way down the hill to the bridge, by which the communication with the town is preserved. The whole hill is covered with camomile. On the preservation or loss of this hill and fort that of the town chiefly depends.

What gave this town so great a name was the fervour and courage of the Protestants, who in the late wars retired into this fastness, as into a camp, and having here formed themselves into regular bodies, issued out against the enemy on all sides. A great number of these gallant men were the inhabitants of Fermanagh ; but beside these there were many others gathered to them from the neighbouring counties of Cavan, Monaghan, Donegal, Leitrim, and a large body of the Protestants of County Sligo, who being treacherously drawn out of the fort of Sligo by Lundy, Governor of Derry, retired hither under the conduct of Col. Lloyd. All these, from the place to which they retired, went by the name of Inniskilleners. These men in all their battles, at Burndroose[1], Newtownbutler[2], Cavan, Boyne, and Aughrim, and several skirmishes, distinguished themselves with an intrepidity and ardour which nothing could withstand ; difficulties and dangers—instead of

---

[1] Or Bundrowse, May, 1689.   [2] On 31 July, 1689 (pp. 27-34).

abating—served only to increase and raise it, and to make them come off the more victorious. It is too low a name to call the spirit wherewith they were animated COURAGE : it was rather a Divine fire kindled in them from above, and kept alive by a just sense of the inestimable value of these two blessings, RELIGION and LIBERTY !

But lest they should imagine it was their own sword and arm that helped them, it pleased God to suffer them to receive a severe stroke at their own doors, and in a place where, of all others, they had the greatest advantage.

In the interim while Col. Lloyd was absent with the chosen body which defeated the Connaught army at Burndroose, and about three days before the battle of Newtownbutler, the Duke of Berwick—according to the plan before mentioned[1]—marched up with a body of horse—wherewith he covered the siege of Derry— in order to attack the Inniskilleners from the north, while the other two armies fell on them from the south and west, he approaching with his body of horse within half a mile of the town to the strong pass of Cornacrea Mill. This is a very narrow pass, and has on the south side Lough Erne, and on the north side a large land lough, three miles in circuit, beyond which is a morassy country : between these two loughs the northern road runs as a tocher ; at the end of the pass next the town stands a strong mill and a few houses ; and a little behind it rises the fort at the end of the town which commands all ; it is evident, from the situation and natural security of this pass, that a few

[1] P. 29.

men placed in the mill and lining the ditches might
defend it against a great army. The Inniskilleners—
on the hearing of the Duke of Berwick's approach—
detached two companies of foot under the command of
Captain McCormack[1]—supported by two troops of horse
—with strict orders not to advance beyond the pass:
had these orders been observed, in all human probability
the success would have answered the design, but these
bold men, not accustomed to the patient manner of
expecting an enemy, no sooner saw the Duke of Berwick's troops appear on the opposite hill, but bounding
at them, as lions to their prey, flew beyond the pass,
and attacked them on the descent of the hill. Here
they fought with the utmost disadvantages—foot, sword
in hand, against horse—the hill, and the weight of an
heavy-armed body descending it, to struggle against—
72 men only against 700! Yet, with all these disadvantages, they stood till they were cut down on the
spot. Of the two companies only eleven men, and
those desperately wounded, returned to the town. The
horse, which were sent to support them, in obedience
to their orders, stopped at the pass, and maintained it
against the Duke of Berwick, who, observing the
intrepidity of these men, and the impracticableness of
the plan which was concerted, returned immediately
back by the way he came. This was an heavy stroke
to the Inniskilleners, and doubly felt by them, inasmuch

[1] Wm. MacCarmick was taken prisoner on this occasion, and
was kindly dealt with by the Duke of Berwick, until released
by Col. Wolseley, about three weeks after. He was one of the
five who first resolved on taking up arms and defending Enniskillen against K. James's forces [the other four being Robert
Clarke (p. 57), Wm. Browning, and Allan Cathcart, subsequently three of the Captains of the Inniskillen forces, and
James Ewart], and author of *A Farther Impartial Account of
the Actions of the Inniskilling Men.*—Lond., 1691.

as it was the first, and most of the men who fell in this engagement were the inhabitants of the town, who were killed in the very sight of their friends and families ; yet the courage of these few was not without a good effect, for it greatly animated all the rest to fight with unparalleled spirit, which appeared   .   .   .   .

FINIS.

APPENDIX I.

Enniskillen in 1611.

" There is a fair and strong wall newly erected of lime and stone 26 feet high with flankers, parapet, and a walk on the top of the wall built by Capt. Wm. Colle (Cole), constable thereof, towards which he had £200 sterling from the king. A fair house begun upon the foundation of the old castle, with other convenient houses for store and munition. The bawn is ditched about with a fair large ditch, and the river on one side with a good drawbridge. The king has three good boats there ready to attend all services. On a large piece of ground which adjoins the fort the captain has built a good timber house, after the English fashion, in which he and his family now dwell."—*State of Ulster Plantation*, 1611.

Three years previously Sir Arthur Chichester notices that " in this county (Fermanagh) there is neither town nor civil habitation. Inishkellin is the fittest place in his opinion for the shire town ; . . . it is now altogether waste and desolate. But that His Majesty has a ward in the castle."

List of the First Provost and Burgesses of Enniskillen, 1612.

The Lord Deputy ordered, 20 Oct., 1612, the Attorney-General to draw forth a fiant of Incorporation of the town of Inishkellin, with the following names :—

" Captaine William Cole, Provost,
1. Sir John Wisher (Wishart), Knt.,
2. Roger Atkinson, Esq.,
3. Robert Calvert, Esq.,
4. Henry Huninges, Esq.,
5. Thomas Barton, Esq.,
6. Edmund Sybthorpe, Gent.,
7. Thomas Shaw,
8. William Hall,
9. Nicholas Ozenbrooke,
10. Alexander Dunbar,
11. Edward Moore,
12. Alexander Wigham,
13. Ferdinando Burfeild,
14. Joseph Walters."

Sir Arthur Chichester appends a note to the above list :—
" These cannot well stand, for those he should name must be
of the town. These are undertakers." A copy of the same
list has " Captaine Roger Atkinson " and " Edward Sipthorpe."
—*Calendar State Papers* (*Irish Series*), 1611-1614.

" THE NAMES OF THE TOWNESMEN OF ENESKILLIN AND THEIR ARMES, A.D. 163—.

Provest,

1.	Frauncis Bird ;	...	...	Sword onely.
2.	Gerrard Wiggan	...	...	,, ,,
3.	David Williams	...	...	,, ,,
4.	Thomas Browning	...	...	,, ,,
5.	Thomas Smith	...	...	Sword and pike.
6.	Andrew Lewis	...	...	Sword onely.
7.	Ralph Pickring	...	...	,, ,,
8.	Andrew Ward	...	...	Sword and pike.
9.	William Johnston	...	...	Sword onely.
10.	John Harrison	...	...	,, ,,
11.	Thomas Little	...	...	Sword and Pike.
12.	Gilbert Johnston	...	...	Sword onely.
13.	William Wheatlow	...	...	Sword and pike.
14.	Thomas Hogg	...	...	Sword onely.
15.	James Johnston	...	...	,, ,,
16.	Mungo Rotherfeild	...	...	Sword and pike.
17.	Thomas Hill	...	...	Sword and callener.
18.	William Orum	...	...	Sword onely.
19.	James M'Kilmay	...	...	Sword and callener.
20.	George Bochonan	...	...	Sword onely.
21.	John Davis ...	...	...	Sword and pike.
22.	Robert King	...	...	Sword onely.
23.	John Amerson	...	...	Sword and callener.
24.	John Ford ...	...	...	Sword and pike.
25.	John Hays ...	...	...	Sword onely.
26.	Richard Nyst	...	...	Sword and pike.
27.	John Padge ...	...	...	,, ,,
28.	William Hogg	...	...	,, ,,
29.	Richard Smyth	...	...	Sword onely.
30.	John Davison	...	...	Sword and callener.
31.	William Boochannan ...	...	,, ,, ,,
32.	John Blany	...	...	,, ,, ,,
33.	John Radcliff	...	...	Pike onely.
34.	John Carroll	...	...	Sword and Halbert.
35.	John Mouse	...	...	,, ,,
36.	David Logan	...	...	Sword onely.
37.	Richard Maior	...	...	No armes.

38.	William Grible	... ...	No armes.
39.	John Frith	... ...	,,
40.	Jeremy Gleene	... ...	,,
41.	John Maxwell	... ...	,,
42.	George Gylesby	... ...	,,
43.	Robert Ree ...	... ...	,,
44.	*Rynyon Watson	... ...	,,
45.	Georg Nichols	... ...	,,
46.	John Caldwell	... ...	,,
47.	Christopher Charleton	...	,,
48.	*Rynyon Armestrong	...	,,
49.	Thomas M'Cartan, younger	...	,,
50.	David Minshaw	... ...	,,
51.	Brian Johnston	... ...	,,
52.	Thomas Yates	... ...	,,

Barony of Magherbuy."

" *The Muster Roll of the county of ffarmanagh.*"—B.M.

* Ninian.

APPENDIX II.

The Inniskilleners.

" The Address sent from Inniskillen by Mr. Andrew Hamilton, and presented to their Majesties at Hampton Court, 12th Oct., 1689.

To their Most Excellent Majesties K. William and Queen Mary.

The humble address of the Governour, Officers, Clergy and other Inhabitants of your Majesties Town of Iniskillin, in your Majesties Kingdom of Ireland.

We, your Majesties most Faithful and most Loyal Subjects, do in the first place offer up unto Almighty God our most humble Thanks for the Deliverance vouchsafed us from our Merciless and Bloody Enemies ; and next unto your most Sacred Majesties, for your gracious care taken of us, and in sending Major-General Kirk to the relief of the poor handful of your Majesties' Protestant Subjects left in this place, and Derry (whose miraculous holding out, under God, has been the preservation of the Protestant interest in this Kingdom), and for those worthy Officers sent to this place by him, among which the Honourable Colonel William Wolsley, our Commander-in-Chief, under whose great and happy conduct God has been pleased to bless us with the most signal and remarkable victory obtained over our enemy, in this or the former age. And as we were early in the demonstration of our loyalty in proclaiming your Most Sacred Majesties, on the eleventh day of March last, so we shall persevere in the same dutiful allegiance to our lives' end, ever imploring the Divine Majesty to continue your prosperous reign long, and long over us, most humbly begging your Most Sacred Majesties favourably to accept this Address of our most humble and sincere obedience, which we shall ever be ready to make good both with our hearts and hands.

Gustavus Hamilton, Govern.
Tho. Lloyd.
Dan. Hodson.
W. Smith.
Morgan Hart.
Allex. Acheson.
Isaac Collyer.
George Dury.
Tho. White.
William Wiseheart.
Robert Moor.
Fran. Folliot.
John Dean.
Fran. Graham.
William Irvine.
Ja. Graham.
Tho. Roscrow.
Andrew Montgomery.
Daniel French.
Henry Smith.
Richard Newstead.
Robert Starling.
Henry Johnston.
Matthew Webster.
William Slack.
Allan Cathcart.
An. Hamilton.
James Johnston.
Ja. Golden.
Arnold Cosbye.
†Jo. Price.
Robert Johnston.
Francis Aldrich.
William Parsons.
Ambrose Bedel.

Tho. Hart.
Edw. Dixy.
Ichabod Skelson. ‡
Hen. Howel.
Robert Stevenson.
Thomas Johnston.
William Johnston.
Thomas Osborn.
Thomas Scot.
John Lowder.
William Kitle.
William Birney.
James King.
† Jo. Rider.
Christopher Carleton.
Ja. Devitt.
Charles mac Fayden.
Lawrence Crow.
Edward Ellis.
William Blashford.
Robert Clark.
William Browning.
Ja. Johnston.
Ja. Browning.
Roger Wilton.
Ed. Wood.
F. King.
Robert Drury.
John Browning.
Ja. Campbell.
George Cashell.
Povey Hookes.
John Armstrong.
Toby Mulloy.
Robert Vaughan.

H. Hughs.
Jason Hazard.
Tho. Hughes.
James Matthews.
Mart. Armstrong.
* Claud. Bealy.
Ninian Scot.
Tho. Armstrong.
Jo. Frisell.
Dan. Armstrong.
Matthew Young.
Marc. Buchanan.
George Wattson.
Ro. MacConnell.
Ja. Robinson.
Jo. Roberts.
Ro. Ward.
Bar. Gibson.
Jo. Crozier.
Hu. Blair.
† Jo. King.
Thomas Young.
John Fulton.
George Hart.
James Matthews.
Ja. Lucy.
Francis Ellis.
Hercules Ellis.
John Corry.
Jo. Neper.
James Corry.
John Sheriffe.
George Corry.
Samuel Forth.
James Cathcart.
Edward Cosbye.
William MacCormick.
William Campbell.
Charles King."

Robert Wear.
Malcolme Cathcart.
Robert Robison.
Hugh Montgomery.
George Cooper.
Hu. Cathcart.
Hugh Corry.
Ed. Davenport.
Au. Ellis.
† Jo. Woodward.
William Gore.
William Charleton.
George Russell.
Aylet Sammes.
Ja. Mitchell.
Mat. Lindsay.
Thomas Davenport.
All. Fulton.
Paul Dean, Provost.
Ja. Ewart.
Jo. Ballard.
Thomas Shore.
Richard Taylor.
Ed. Gubbin.
§ Thomas Leturvel.
George Hamersley.
William Frith.
† Jo. Hall.
Robert Johnston.
Cor. Donnellan.
Theo. Bury.
Hu. Galbraith.
William Ross.
John Galbraith.
Matthew Young.
James Delap.
William Ball.
Jo. Smith."

‡ Skelton.   * Beaty?   § Latournel.

† " Jo " was an old abbreviation for *John*, and not, as now, for *Joseph*.

A True Relation of the Actions of the Inniskilling-Men.
By ANDREW HAMILTON, Rector of Kilskerrie, &c.
Lond. 1690.

" BRIGADIER WM. WOLSELY'S REGT. OF HORSE,
BROKE IN IRELAND, 1698.
(Add. MSS. 9762.—B.M.)

				New Subsist. p. annum.		
				£	s.	d.
Field Officers	Lieut. Coll. Wm. Berry, 3/-, and as Capt. 7/-	...	...	146	0	0
	Major Thom⁸ Price	...	...	127	15	0
Captaines	Richard Wolsely	...	...	91	5	0
	Francis Folliot ...	...	...	91	5	0
	John Auchmooty	...	...	91	5	0
	Wm. Blashfort ...	...	...	91	5	0
Lievtenants	Samll Forth	...	...	54	15	0
	James Johnson¹...	...	...	54	15	0
	John Green	...	...	54	15	0
	John Deane	...	...	54	15	0
	Robt. Johnson¹ ...	...	...	54	15	0
	Lanc⁺ Irwyn	...	...	54	15	0
Cornetts	Thom. Featherston	...	...	45	12	6
	Richd Berry	...	...	45	12	6
	James Cathcart	...	...	45	12	6
	Peter Sandys	...	...	45	12	6
	Daniel Harford ...	...	...	45	12	6
	Lanc⁺ Carlton	...	...	45	12	6
Quarter Mⁿˢ	Thos. Wingfield ...	...	...	27	7	6
	James Humphrys	...	...	27	7	6
	Henry Dixon	...	...	27	7	6
	Francis Aldrige ...	...	...	27	7	6
	Michˡ Waldron ...	...	...	27	7	6
	Gerard Irwyn	...	...	27	7	6
Adjutant ...	Herbert Price	...	...	36	10	0

Note 1.—In Half Pay List, 24 Oct. 1699, "Johnston."

" COLL. ABRAH. CREIGHTON'S REGT. OF FOOTE,
BROKE IN IRELAND, 1698.

			New Subsist. p. annum.		
			£	s.	d.
Field Officers	Abraham Creighton as Coll. att 5/-, and as Capt. 4/-	146	0	0(?)
	Juº Caufield as Liev⁺ Coll. at 2/6, and as Capt. 4/-	109	10	0
	Malch. Hamilton as Major at 1/8, and as Capt. 4/-	91	5	0

				New Subsist. p. annum.		
				£	s.	d.
Captaines	George Brooks[1]	...	...	54	15	0
	——— ——— Vacant[2]					
	David Creighton	...	...	54	15	0
	Abra. Green[3] ...	...	...	54	15	0
	Wm. Browning	...	...	54	15	0
	Alex. Achison	...	...	54	15	0
	Francis Johnston	...	...	54	15	0
	Thom^{s} Johnston, Junr	...	...	54	15	0
	Mich. Cole ...	...	...	54	15	0
	James Browning	...	...	54	15	0
Lievtenants	John Orban ...	...	...	36	10	0
	Richd. Arbuthnett	...	...	36	10	0
	George Hewson[4]	...	...	36	10	0
	George Corry[5]	...	...	36	10	0
	Robert Montgomry	...	...	36	10	0
	Guy Carlton ...	...	...	36	10	0
	Francis Green[3]	...	...	36	10	0
	George Graham	...	...	36	10	0
	Alex^{r} Fulton	...	...	36	10	0
	George Johnston	...	...	36	10	0
	Ralph Picken[6]	...	...	36	10	0
	James Devitt[7]	...	...	36	10	0
	Gabriell Shore	...	...	36	10	0
	George Cashill[8]	...	...	36	10	0
Ensignes	Jn° Creighton	...	...	27	7	6
	Henry Cosby ...	...	...	27	7	6
	Jn° Armstrong	...	...	27	7	6
	Edwd. Napper	...	...	27	7	6
	Jn° Johnston[9]	...	...	27	7	6
	Henry Hodkinson[10]	...	...	27	7	6
	Thos Vincent	...	...	27	7	6
	Jn° Browning	...	...	27	7	6
	Jas. Laynge[11]	...	...	27	7	6
	Mau Buchanon[12]	...	...	27	7	6
	Jn° Johnston[13]	...	...	27	7	6
	Wm. Hamilton	...	...	27	7	6
Staff Officers	Luke Davis as Adjutant[14]		...	36	10	0
	Thos. Little, Quarter M^{r}		...	36	10	0

NOTE.

In Half Pay List, 24 Oct. 1699—

[1] "Brook;"   [2] vacancy filled by Jas. Trailboy;   [3] "Greene;"
[4] "Houston;"   [5] "Curry;"   [6] "Pickin;"   [7] "Devet;"   [8] "Cashell;"
[9] "John Johnston, Senr.;"   [10] "Hodgkinson;"   [11] "Lainge;"   [12] "Maurice Buchanon;"   [13] "Jn° Johnston, Junr.;"   [14] "Adjutant Clarke."

"OFFICERS OF BRIG^R TIFFIN'S REGIMENT DISBANDED.

> Captain Henry Cookeman.
> Captain John Woodwart.
> Lt. Leonard Thickpenny.
> Lt. Thomas Keire.
> Ens^n Andrew Singleton.
> Ens^n Henry Gore."

THE GREAT FIRE IN ENNISKILLEN, JUNE 2, 1705.

"IN the year 1705 the place was almost wholly destroyed by fire, 'whereby 114 families and their servants suffered very severe losses, and the barrack of her Majesty with all the utensils thereto belonging sustained great damage.' In consequence of this great public calamity, a memorial was presented to the Duke of Ormond, then Lord Lieutenant, on behalf of the sufferers to grant them the benefit of public collections; in this the memorialists declare,—

"That ye Petrs. have been very much decayed and lessened in their substance, not only by the maintaining many thousands of poor stript Protestants, who came for protection in the late Rebellion, but several terrible fires that have happened in the said Town, particularly one that happened on Saturday the 2nd of June inst., which has to a very small matter, reduced the whole Town to ashes; and was so sudden and violent, that they saved little or nothing of their household goods and other effects, so that they have (by the best computation) lost to the value of £8,000."

This proposed collection from 'house to house throughout the kingdom, and in all Cathedrals and parish churches' was approved by the Lord Lieutenant, and ordered to continue in force in Ireland for a year from the 23rd of June, 1705; the Bp. of Clogher and Capt. James Corry, of Castlecoole, M.P., were appointed trustees of the fund.—Canon Bradshaw's *Enniskillen Long Ago*, 1878.

In order to obtain a Brief from the Crown authorizing public collections for the same object in England, Sir Michael Cole applied to the Abp. of Dublin, and the following letters on the subject were written, and have been printed in *Parliamentary Memoirs of Tyrone*, 1887:—

* " PALL MALL, *Augt.* 3rd, 1705.

S^R

I rec^d a letter from you when I was at Tunbridge about Iniskillin, as soon as I came to town I waited on his Grace the Duke of Ormond, he told me he had spoke to the Queen about the affair, and was in hopes to p'cure a brief in England. He said if I remember right that Corry the Knight for the Shire had press'd him much in it, and he had engaged to him to do his best, and Mr. Portlock, his Secretary, told me the same again. I left a memorial with Mr. Portlock for his Grace, and (he) seems zealous in it ; My Ld. ordered me to do so. I am of opinion that you shou'd if possible wait on his Grace, and make him sensible of the case of that poor town, for none can do it more feelingly nor has a better title to do it. I have heard that there was some contest amongst the people, whom they shou'd employ about this matter. 'Tis necessary to pitch on p'sons that will be gratefull (*i.e.*, acceptable) to the Duke his Grace, for if anything be obtained it must be by him. I give you this hint because a little mistake may spoil all. My respects to my Ldy.

I recommend you to Gd., and am &c.,

W. DUBLIN.

S^R MICHAEL COLE, Egham
near Stains, Middlesex."

* " TUNBRIDGE WELLS, *Aug.* 12, 1705.

MAY IT PLEASE YOUR GRACE,

I mentioned to your Grace the affair of Iniskillin and found your Grace well appris'd of it, the bearer Sr. Gustavus Hume, is employed by the miserable inhabitants to rep'sent their condition to your Grace and solicite your Grace's favour in their behalf. He is a Gentleman that has an Estate in the neighbourhood of the Town and has bin an eye witness of the miserable condition of it. The sight of which together with their importunity has p'vailed on him to undertake this journey. They entirely depend on your Grace's mediation to procure a Brief for them here in England, or such other assistance as her Majesty shall think fitt. I find he is sensible how forward your Grace was to favour them, and I told him that I hoped there wou'd be nothing else for him to do but to acknowledge in the name of those that sent him, your Grace's goodness in so readily espousing their interest. He believes my letter may help to

* " *MSS. King Correspondence, penes Sir C. S. King, Bt.*"

introduce him to your Grace, which occasions the trouble of
this to your Grace, which I hope your Grace will pardon. All
the return your Grace must expect for this and the many good
offices you have done for Ireland, are the pray[rs] and acknow-
ledgments of all concerned for its welfare, and more particularly
of

My Lord

Your Grace's, &c.,

W. DUBLIN.

To

HIS GRACE THE DUKE OF ORMOND."

The writer of the above letters was William King, Scholar,
Trin. Coll. Dub., 1667 ; D.D., 1688 : Provost of Tuam, 1676 ;
Chancellor of St. Patrick's, 1679, and Dean, 1689. Having
become obnoxious to K. James's party through his zeal for the
Protestant faith and his opposition to the extension of the royal
prerogative, he was closely confined in the Bermingham Tower,
Dublin Castle, 29 July to December, 1689, and again in 1690 ;
he also narrowly escaped assassination, and at this period, in
the words of Lord Macaulay, "no Protestant divine suffered
more hardships." For his great sufferings and services in promoting the Revolution, he was raised to the See of Derry, and
consecrated 25 January, 169$\frac{9}{7}$. Translated to the Archbishopric
of Dublin, 11 March, 170$\frac{2}{3}$. A Lord Justice, 1714, 1716, 1717,
and 1722. Author of *The State of the Protestants of Ireland
under King James's Government* (1691), the learned treatise,
De Origine Mali (1702), several sermons and controversial
works of less note, besides an extensive correspondence on the
various questions of the day with the leading men of his time.
Died 1729, unmarried. Dean Swift thus winds up a long eulogy
on this Archbishop's character and public actions. "This and
more, if possible, is due to so excellent a person, who may be
justly reckoned among the greatest and most learned prelates
of this age."

His father, who settled first in Co. Antrim, and in 1658, in
Tyrone, was a Scot of the same stock as the Fermanagh
family (p. 56), "Ipse natus Calendis Maii, 1650, patre Jacobo,
ejusdem nominis avo et proavo, familiâ antiqua generosa de
Burras in Scotiâ Septentrionali " (*Quædam vitæ meæ insigniora*,
MS. by Abp. King), and though a rigid Presbyterian, would not
engage in the Solemn League and Covenant at that time im-
posed in Ulster under a species of excommunication ; the future
Archbishop's baptism was consequently delayed for six months,
until, in the absence of his father at the war, his friends had the
ordinance performed.

APPENDIX III.

"List of Crown Tenants in Fermanagh, Rental for 1678.*"

A.

Aldridge, Edwd.
Allen, Stephen.
Anckitell, Mathew.
Archdale, Wm.
Atkinson, Roger.
Austin, John.

B.

Ob. Oct. 1634.

Ob. 1639.

Balfour, James, Lord.
Baxter, Martin.
Blennerhassett, Sir Leonard,
    ,,   Francis. [Knt.
    ,,   William.
Brooke, Sir Henry, Knt.
Bull, Samuel.
Butler, Francis.

C.

One of the 1649 officers, ob. 1666.

One of the '49 officers.

Caldwell, James.
Carew, Robert.
Cathcart, Adam.
Champion, Arthur.
    ,,   Edward.
Cheslen, John.
Claneboy, James, Lord.
Cock, Francis.
Cole, Sir John, Bart.
    ,,   Sir Michael, Knt.

* " I have modernized the spelling of names, and placed them in more correct alphabetical order.—C. S. King."

Note by Lord Belmore.—" It does not follow that all these persons were alive in 1678. For instance, Roger Atkinson was probably dead. He had sold his grant long before to Arthur Champion, and it was now held by John Corry, in addition to another for which his own name appears ; but the names were kept on in the Rental."

College, Dublin.
Connyes, Edward.
Copeland, Edward.
Ob. 1660-1.   Cormuck, John.
Corry, John.

D.

Dillon, Robert, Lord.
  ,,   Carey.
  ,,   Charles.
Dunbar, Sir John, Knt.

E.

Evett, Margaret.
  ,,   Richard.

F.

Folliot, Thomas, Lord.
Ob. 1686-8.   Forster, Arthur.
Francklin, Richard.

G.

Gore, Sir Ralph, Bart.

H.

Hamilton, John.
  ,,   Malcolm.
Hannington, Maria.
Harrison, George.
Ob. 1690.   Hassard, Jason.
Hastings, Ferdinando, Lord.
Lucy, d. of Sir John Davis.   ,, and Lucy, his wife.
Archd. of Ardagh, Ob. 1632.   Hatton, Edward.
A son of Bp. Heygate.   Heygate, John.
Hume, Sir Geo., Bart.
Humphrey, Thos.

I.

Irvine, Gerard.

J.

One of the '49 officers, ob. 1693.   Johnston, Walter.
Jones, Roger.

K.

Vivens 1674.   King, James.

L.

Ob. July, 1681.
Ob. Feb., 1700.

Leonard, John.
Leslie, John, Dr. of Theolog.
Lowther, Henry, Assign Henry
Lowther.

M.

Mackie, Thomas.
Maguire, Lord.
    ,,   Bryan M'Coron.

One of the '49 officers.

Ob. 1692.

Merrick, Richard.
Monmouth, Jas., Duke of
Montgomery, Gabriel.
    ,,   William.
Mountmorris, Francis, Lord.

O.

O'Neil, Art Oge.

P.

Peirce, Ralph.
Pitt, John.
Potter, George.
Puckridge, Richard.

R.

Ob. Nov. 1677.

Rhynd, David.
Roscommon, Jas., Earl of.
Rotheram, Sir Thos. (Knt. ?)

S.

Vivens, 1634.

Slack, Robert, Clk.
St. George, George.

W.

Ob. 1638.

Vivens 1621.

Walmesley, John.
Waterhouse, Charles.
West, Henry.
Willoughby, Nicholas.
Wyett, Dr. Thomas."

Parliamentary Memoirs of Fermanagh and Tyrone.   1887.
By the EARL OF BELMORE.

THE PRINCIPAL BRITISH FAMILIES IN

FERMANAGH IN 1718.*

The following appeared in *Notes and Queries*, 4 Oct.,
1879 :—

" MS. Hist. of Fermanagh. Following a friend's suggestion,
I searched the library catalogue at Thirlestane House, Cheltenham, and found the above at p. 238 (No. 13293). It is entitled
*History of the County of Fermanagh, with the Antient Families
of the Same.* It is a small 4to of 165 pp., written 1718-19. The
contents comprise a description of the town of Enniskillen, the
islands, hills, and mountains in the county, the ancient Irish
families, *e.g.*, Maguires, MacManuses, Cassidys, &c., and the
principal British families. The list of names of the heads of
the latter, comprising the landed gentry of the Co. 160 years
ago, will doubtless interest many readers of ' N. & Q.' :—

" An Alphabetical Table of ye most Remarkable Brittish
families in ye County of Fermanagh, proceeding according to y^e
first letter of each sirname, wherein by ye pages annexed to their
names ye description may be found in ye book at ye same page.

William Archdale, Esqr. ; Marvin Archdale, Coll. ; Mr. Alexander Acheson, Gt. ; Mr. James Aghinleck ; Mr. Robt. Aber-
crumbey.

Wm. Balfoure, Esqr. ; Henry Brook, Esqr.

John Cole, Esqr. ; Henry Caldwell, Barrt. ; David Creichton,
Esqr. ; John Corry, Esqr. ; John Creichton, Esqr. ; Guy Carle-
ton, Esqr. ; Malcolm Cathcart, Esqr. ; Allan Cathcart, Esqr. ;
Mr. John Cochran, Gent.

John Dunbair, Esqr. ; Mr. Henry Dunbair, Gent.

Gilbert Ecles, Esqr.; Joseph Ecles, Esqr.

Arthur Forster, Gent.

Sir Ralph Gore, Barrt. ; Mr. Willm. Graton, Clk. ; Mr. Wm.
Green, Clk. ; Mr. Henry Green, Attorney.

Sir Gustavus Hume, Barrt. ; Lodovick Hamilton, Gent. ;
Malcolm Hamilton, Gent. ; Capt. Charles Hamilton ; Jason
Hassard, Esqr. ; Robert Hassard, High Sheriff ; Thomas Hum-
frey, Gent.

* From Dr. Samuel Madden's MS. *Hist. of Co. Fermanagh.*

Christopher Irvin, Esqr.; James Johnston, Esqr.; Walter Johnston, Esqr.; James Johnston, Esqr.

John King, Gent.

Edward Leonard, Gent.; Anthony Luige, Gent.

Hugh Montgomery, Esqr.; Samuel Madden, Esq.; Andrew Mitchell, Clk.; John Means, Gent.; Peter Madison, Gent.

Arthur Noble, Majr.; James Noble, Gent.; Edwd. Noble, Gent.; Thomas Nixon, Gent.

David Rynd, Esqr.; John Rynd, Esqr.; Mr. Willm. Rossgrove, Gent.; Mr. Thos. Rossgrove, Gent.

Mr. John Smith, Clk., Esqr.; Mr. Thos. Smith, Gent.

Mr. John Tratter, Gent.

Hugh Willoghbey, Esqr.; Mr. John Wisheart, Gent.; Mr. Robt. Wier, Gent.; Nicholas Ward, Esqr.; John Winslow, Esqr."

The majority of the above seem from their surnames to have been of Scottish origin.

C. S. K."

Kensington."

APPENDIX IV.

Knockninny Hill.

" In this County (Fermanagh) are two notable hills for beauty, pleasure, profitt, and stately situation not inferior to many in Ireland the one[1] is called Knockninny being the principall seate of that family descended of Patrick son of Edmond na Cooley Maguire, king of ffermanagh. This hill is bordering upon Lough Earne on ye weast side about 10 miles from Iniskellin and 8 miles from ye town of Beltorbet, the waters of Lough-earne encompasseth one side of this hill ab^t an English mile, being on all sides bordered and adorned wth fine stately groves of smale woods plenty of heasle nutts, slows and crabbs, or wild apples, and on ye faces of this hill groweth wheat, beare, barley, flax or any other graine most plentiful. The meddows and pastures round this hill excellent for tillege and pleasant

---

[1] " The second hill for beauty and profit is called Cravbh in ye east end of Tirkenedy, being part of the estate belonging to ye heirs of Cuchonaght More Maguire."

and wholesome soyle for man or beast. The height of this hill is most stately to behold being adorned with desyes and all kind of sweete smelling and wholesome herbs, very usefull for appothecaries, as also the pleasantest prospect in y⁰ County for one may see from thence all y⁰ stately buildings in y⁰ Co., as also y⁰ Boates and Cotts yᵗ goes by water from Iniskillin to Beltorbet, being 20 miles by water, there being severall other recreations which makes this hill most famous, as at y⁰ foot thereof may be found a salmon, a peyk, a breame, and a trout, and on yᵉ hill and borders a fox, a hare, a badger, and sometimes a deere, besides good fowleing, soe yᵗ Nature hath fortified and hon'red this place above all other hills in our Northern ptes."—MS. *Hist. of Fermanagh*, 1718, 1719.

———————————

We are strangers before Thee, and sojourners, as all our fathers were. Our days on the earth are as a shadow, and there is no abiding.—I CHRON. xxix. 15, R.V.

———————————

INDEX.

Names of Families, Places, &c., not mentioned by the Author, but which appear in the Editor's notes, are printed in *italics*.

C. W. GIBBS, Printer, 18 Wicklow Street, Dublin.